The Flying Fisherman

Gone Fishin'

The Flying Fisherman

by

R.V. "Gadabout" Gaddis

as told to
George Sullivan

PUBLISHED BY POCKET BOOKS NEW YORK

THE FLYING FISHERMAN

Trident Press edition published January, 1967

A *Pocket Book* edition

1st printing

This *Pocket Book* edition includes every word
contained in the original, higher-priced edition. It is printed
from brand-new plates made from completely reset, clear, easy-to-read
type. *Pocket Book* editions are published by Pocket Books, a division
of Simon & Schuster, Inc., 630 Fifth Avenue, New York, N.Y. 10020.
Trademarks registered in the United States and other countries.

L

To
Winston Mergott

Contents

The Flying Fisherman

1. All in a Day's Fun

THE LUSH NEW ENGLAND COUNTRYSIDE DRIFTED BY SERENELY below.

I was cruising at 7,500 feet in a cloudless spring sky and at peace with mankind.

Mister, I was doing what I love best in this world: flying my little Piper Cherokee between fishing holes.

I had wrapped up some bow fishing for long-nosed gar on the Santee-Cooper Lakes in South Carolina that morning. By sundown I'd be wet fly fishing for rainbow trout on the Kennebec River in Maine.

I was basking in two delights: the satisfaction of having wound up another episode for my television series and the anticipation of getting down to some serious vacationing.

This old boy was as content as a lazy hound dog snoozing under a porch out of the noonday sun.

Then it happened.

One second I was gazing ahead at the Rhode Island-Massachusetts border just east of Providence. The next instant there was nothing—a pitch blackness as though someone had tossed a king-sized shroud over the world.

"My Lord," I thought. "I've gone blind!"

A second later I was laughing at myself—almost.

What was happening was that black, sticky oil was gushing from a seam in the hood and being driven against the windshield by 75 pounds of oil line pressure and by the propwash of a propeller doing 2,300 revolutions per minute.

My second thought was a lot clearer than the first. I killed the motor to reduce the chance of fire.

Now I was on a dead stick.

I was in a fix and knew it. But I also knew I was a lucky, lucky man for at least two good reasons.

One was that I had at least two excellent airfields within 15-mile range either way—Providence to the southwest, New Bedford to the northeast. The other was that I was at good gliding altitude, riding a healthy tailwind and figured to be able to make either port.

1

Now I had a split-second decision: Providence or New Bedford?

I picked New Bedford. It was slightly closer. It was also almost dead ahead and wouldn't require about-face maneuvering with a powerless engine and the limited vision that Providence would. And finally New Bedford figured to have less traffic.

I radioed New Bedford tower.

Now this wasn't any Hollywood drama with Maydays and appeals for fire trucks to stand by. I merely told the tower my position and my predicament.

The operator asked if I thought I could make it and I said I did.

The tower cleared all traffic and told me to take any runway I wanted because ground wind was only seven or eight knots.

Meanwhile all I could do was pray I didn't run out of altitude. That ground was coming up closer every second.

Yes, sir, I did a little praying. There was a saying during World War II that there are no atheists in fox holes. Let me tell you there aren't any holding dead sticks in crippled aircraft, either.

The old ticker was throbbing a bit.

Finally the airfield popped into view—the sweetest sight these eyes ever feasted on.

Now all I had to do was land my ship frontwards while looking sideways.

I had just enough height remaining to make a left turn and approach Runway 5, giving me a chance to survey the strip. I lined up the runway and started in slightly parallel to it.

100 feet . . . 50 . . . 25.

All the while I kept the edge of the runway in view as I floated over the grass next to it and made as sure as I could that I had it lined up perfectly.

Fifteen feet—the moment of truth.

I eased the ship over where I figured the asphalt to be and set down blindly.

Touchdown—I was home safe!

Well, sir, to shorten a long story, the trouble turned out to be a tiny sand hole in the oil line—the biggest little flaw I ever saw. But with 75 pounds of pressure behind it, it might as well have been a fire hose.

A couple of mechanics fixed it up pronto.

2

By sunset I was hooking me a fat and sassy rainbow on the Kennebec.

It was all in a day's fun for Gadabout Gaddis The Flying Fisherman.

2. *Gone Fishin'*

Little Cove Lane
Old Greenwich,
Connecticut

Dear Mr. Gaddis:

Like his father, my eight-year-old son thinks your television show is tops.

Coming to pick me up at work one day, he said to his mother, "You won't have to worry about spending money on me for college."

She asked why.

"You don't have to go to college to be a fisherman, do you?" he replied.

"No, Bob," she said. "But you might want to go to college so you can make money for your family."

"Did Gadabout Gaddis go to college?" Bob asked.

"I don't know, Bob," his mother answered. "But not many people can make money while fishing like Mr. Gaddis does."

"Well," persisted the young entrepreneur, "Gadabout is getting pretty old, and when he dies I'll be ready to take over his program."

Brother, this portion of a letter from a perplexed father named Russ DeWaard really tore me up. I mean it really tickled me.

Of all the thousands and thousands of letters I receive, none has ever been so flattering in a wonderful, unaffected way. And none has hit upon something else more squarely.

Everybody thinks old Gadabout has life made.

3

I hear from Army generals, doctors, lawyers, bankers and just plain Joes telling me the exact same thing.

Not too long ago, Johnny Strauss collared me in Hollywood. He's with MacFadden, Strauss, Eddy and Irwin, who handle public relations for a lot of movie stars.

"Fred MacMurray wants to meet you," he said.

"Well, I'd like to meet Mr. MacMurray too," I said. "I admire his acting very much in the movies and on television. He must have quite a life."

"That's just it," said Johnny. "He thinks *you* are the one who has it made."

And so it goes.

Everyone thinks I'm the luckiest person God ever created.

About twenty million people look into their picture boxes each week, shake their heads and say, "How lucky can a guy be? Imagine getting paid for living that life of Riley? That old boy really has it made!"

Well, sir, I have to agree with them. I *do* have it made. I'd be fibbing if I tried to deny it.

I'm doing exactly what I always wanted to do: fish and gallivant.

And I've been doing it most of my life.

I hung out the "Gone Fishin'" sign almost sixty-five years ago and have been gone just about ever since.

You can believe me or not, but over the last fifty-five years, I can't remember ever having spent thirty consecutive nights under one roof.

I've had the hankering to roam since I could walk; to fish since I was seven.

Except for a few remote childhood fancies, I've never really wanted to do anything else. And so I haven't done anything else. It's as simple and confounded as that.

Of course I didn't set out to be on television or anything like that when I was a kid. Heck, I was invented long before TV was—or even radio. What I mean is that I loved fishing from the first time I put a line in the water, and it wasn't long after that I made up my mind that I was going to make a living out of it somehow someday.

I could have gone into other things over the years. But I never could pry myself away. Actually I was beyond temptation. I'm lazy by nature and was having too much fun—and still am.

And my wandering fit in with the fishing perfectly. In all

4

my travels, I never knew what I was looking for. I still can't explain it today. All I know is that it was something that I had to do. I had to keep on the move like a man one step ahead of a sheriff.

If you offered me $1,000,000 on the barrelhead, I couldn't name you all the places I've lived. I mean it. I've maintained a home in Florida over the years. But I never spent more than a few days a year there. I'm too busy traveling—anywhere, everywhere.

Between roaming and fishing, there aren't many bodies of water I've missed from coast to coast. I have fished in every state except Hawaii in this great country of ours—and in a couple territories outside our borders.

I've been lucky—tremendously lucky.

Just the fact I've managed to live through seventy years and still feel as frisky as a pinto pony is proof enough of that.

It's been a wonderful, wonderful life—even in the days when I didn't have any more than a nickel in my pocket.

Wonderful? Mister, it's been the darndest life any three men together could ever have.

3. The Mold Is Cast

I'M A GADABOUT BY BIRTH AS WELL AS BY NATURE.

Between the day I was born and my seventeenth birthday, my folks lived in seven towns spread across five states.

George Gaddis & family pitched their tent in Mattoon, Illinois; Greenville, Mississippi; Shelbyville, Indiana; Owensboro, Kentucky; Madison, Indiana; Great Falls, Montana; and Paducah, Kentucky.

The longest we ever stayed in one place was six years—in Mattoon, where I was born on January 28, 1896.

The other stops averaged just over two years—just about the amount of time it took to build a gas house and set its gears in motion back at the turn of the century. And that's exactly what my dad did for a living. He was a construction engineer who specialized in building gas plants.

5

My memories of some of those times and places are fuzzy.

But two recollections stick out crystal clear in my mind: the urge to wander—and getting a switch across my bottom plenty for it.

My first fish—a one-pound catfish.

Maybe Mr. Freud would have something to say about that. I mean I'm still doing the same things today, roaming and fishing. The only difference is that I'm getting paid instead of paddled for them.

So I doubt it's coincidence that I remember those happenings so clearly. They took place while I was still walking bowlegged. But they pretty much cast the mold for my life.

Let me bend your ear a bit about it.

4. The Urge to Roam

"ROSCOE! WHERE *are* YOU, ROSCOE!"

The voice still echoes clearly in my memory after all these years. It was that of my mother trying to fetch me from the nooks and crannies of an eastern Illinois wonderland named Mattoon.

I was the first-born of George and Minnie Gaddis. Lillian, Raymond, Irene and Dorothy would follow me in years to come. And it's well I headed the parade. Till the day she died, mom delighted in telling—with just a dash of unforgotten grief —how the good Lord had blessed her by sending me first. I was a handful by myself without having anyone else to look after.

She'd tell how I was a roamer almost from the day I took my first steps. I always had to find out what was in the next room, the next yard, the next street.

I got myself lost for the first time when I was exactly two years old. Mom found me wandering along the railroad tracks on the edge of town.

She warmed my backside good for it. Dad was a big man— about 6-2, 220—and a rough man among men. And he was a firm customer at home when he had to be. But at this time he left most of the disciplining to mom, a medium-sized

6

woman and usually a quiet and happy one—except when she was weary and frantic from chasing Roscoe.

Let me explain something about my name right here and now.

I was christened Roscoe Vernon Gaddis. Where my folks picked up those handles I'll never know. Even they couldn't explain it in later years. They weren't family names. And it wasn't because I was of German and Irish descent. I've looked up the names, and neither is of those origins that I can find.

Whatever the reason, I was stuck with them. Thankfully, no one ever called me Roscoe except mother. To everyone else I was Vernon as a kid. Later it would be shortened to "Vern." And still later I picked up "Gad"—first as short for Gaddis, then as short for gadabout.

Anyway, mom walloped me pretty good for getting lost that first time. She could have saved her effort. Inside a month I had gotten lost a second time in a little swamp on the other side of town.

Mister, talk about your lost lamb!

I mean that woman was always looking for me around the neighborhood. Sometimes even before she had a chance to know I was gone, somebody would be bringing me back or I'd be ringing the doorbell myself. Mom even got so desperate that she started tieing me with a long rope to a tree in the backyard. That didn't do much good either. In no time I'd have the knots untied somehow and be on my way.

Now who can tell what was going through a two-year-old's mind to make him stroll like that? I sure can't explain it. You just have to chalk it off to roving blood I guess, like a hound who loves his master but takes off anyway once he's let loose.

Looking back on it, though, Mattoon was a town to trigger a youngster's prowling instincts. At the turn of the century it was a farming community of about ten thousand smack in the middle of the prairie. It was a wonderful place to wander about, from the blacksmith's shop in the village to the broomcorn and wheat fields on the outskirts.

It held all sorts of wonders for a pre-school youngster.

I wasn't a farmer's son like most of the other boys. But I might as well have been one. By the time I was five I had spent enough time on a little farm on the edge of town belonging to our next-door neighbors, the Smiths. They had four youngsters: Joe, George, Ova and Frances, and many is the row of corn and beans I hoed with them.

What probably intrigued me about that farm was not so much its contents but its location. It was a couple of miles from our house. That meant travel—not far, but travel all the same.

So you can imagine my excitement when dad used to take mom and me visiting relatives. My grandparents and a lot of aunts and uncles had farms within a 15-mile radius of Mattoon.

We'd often go out for a weekend. When dad would tell me we were going, it was a real thrill. If he made the mistake of telling me at midweek, I couldn't sleep for days in anticipation. Then, on Saturday morning, dad would hitch up a pair of horses to the surrey (yes, sir, with the fringe on top) for the long ride out.

My favorite place of all was Uncle Leige's farm about 10 miles away in a village called Cook's Mills.

Uncle Leige was quite a man. Now there's a real midwestern name for you: Leige Whittley. And uncle was a real midwesterner. He was an erect man who stood about 6-4 and always wore a smile on his face. And not only was he a wonderful, happy man to be around, but he had a houseful of kids—six boys and four girls.

A visit there would mean a real holiday.

I was always well fed at home. And mom was a born cook who knew how to prepare anything and everything—especially the most tempting hot muffins and strawberry shortcake a boy ever tasted.

But the table at Uncle Leige's was something else again. Every day was Thanksgiving. One thing farm folks don't know how to do is skimp on food. And with a herd of kids, the Whittleys put out a spread hearty enough to feed a troop of soldiers. I mean it. But somehow we young ones managed to consume it without much difficulty.

Just about everything at Uncle Leige's place smacked of a flavor to fill a youngster's every curiosity.

It was tailor-made for an investigator like me. It had acres and acres of corn and wheat fields to prowl. There were plenty of domestic animals to see and wild rabbits scooting every which way. And there were all sorts of barns and coops to rummage through.

It also had a little stream called the Okaw River running smack through the middle of it.

8

5. Grandma Was a Fisherman

ONE SPRING MORNING I HEARD MY GRANDMA FLYNN AND Uncle Leige whispering in the kitchen.

"Think he's old enough?" Leige asked.

"He's seven—plenty old enough," grandma said.

I played on the porch and wondered what all the fuss was about.

The years had rolled by. We had already spent a year in Greenville, Mississippi, and had returned to Mattoon. My mother had taken ill for a short spell and my grandmother had dropped by to look after things.

Let me tell you a bit about Grandma Flynn.

There was some woman for you. She was just a marvelous old girl—tiny but chock full of energy and humor.

Grandma knew how to keep a youngster entertained. She was a fabulous story-teller and would keep me spellbound with her yarns. She had traveled by covered wagon from Kentucky with her husband as a young woman and they had helped settle the area around Mattoon when it was still swampland.

To this day I've never forgotten the stories she told about it.

And I've never forgotten what happened that morning at Uncle Leige's place either.

Grandma spotted me peering through the screen door.

"Just the gentleman I'm looking for," she said. "Young fellow, you and I are going to have some fun."

That's when I discovered that besides being full of the dickens and the greatest grandmother a boy ever had, Amanda Flynn was also an incurable fisherman.

Well, sir, she grabbed me by a hand as she exploded out the door and half dragged me along.

"C'mon, Vernon," she said. "Time's a wastin'!"

First we stopped by the garden and dug up some worms. Then we swung by one of the sheds and picked up a couple of cane poles, two hooks, and some twine and cork.

The next stop: the Okaw.

Grandma showed me how to bait a hook and gave me some quick instructions.

9

"Remember, Vernon," she said. "When that cork starts bobbin', don't you yank at it. Draw your catch in easy-like. If you do, you'll get yourself a nice big catfish."

Grandma made a priceless picture. If I live to be a hundred, I'll never forget the sight of her perched on top of a big rock in her great skirts and bonnet and hanging onto that big bamboo pole—every bit a lady.

And I'll never forget either my thrill a short time later when I saw that cork begin to dance on my line.

I got so excited and yanked so hard that I threw that poor catfish back over my head and darn near into the next county. I raced after it like I thought it was going to run off somewhere.

It was worth the chase. There among some weeds was the most beautiful fish I've ever seen in my life: a little catfish that weighed no more than a pound tops. But it was *my* fish—my *first* fish. There is not another thrill like it, especially to a seven-year-old.

Between delight and pride, I thought I was going to bust.

And that was just the beginning. Grandma and I had ourselves quite a morning, taking in six or seven more catfish before finally quitting. We took our prizes back home and grandma skinned them, dressed them and fried them for lunch. And I have never relished a meal to this day as I did that one.

Well, that was that. Grandma had hooked me just as sure as she had hooked any one of those catfish. And she paid the price too. From then on I pestered the daylights out of her to take me fishing.

"C'mon, grandma," I'd badger. "Let's go!"

And I mean every day.

Of course you didn't have to twist Amanda Flynn's arm when it came to fishing and she took me every chance she got.

A whole new world had opened up to me—something very special.

And I couldn't get enough of it.

6. The Gallivanting Gaddises

A MAN PLAYS AN ASSOCIATION GAME WITH HIS MEMORY WHEN he tries to recall events that occurred more than a half-century before in his life.

It's an old game. One person gives a word and the other says the first thing that comes to mind. You know: "black"—"white"; "cat"—"dog"; "money"—"women." It's all reaction.

Let me try it as I attempt to bring back those years between ages seven to thirteen when the Gaddis family was gallivanting around the country as dad constructed one gas house after another.

Mention Greenville, Mississippi, and I recall falling for that town in a big way within an hour of our arrival. I was investigating the back porch of our rented home, which was about five feet from the ground, and—zing-o!—a wasp stung me below an eye and knocked me off balance and clear over the railing. Luckily nothing was seriously hurt other than my pride.

Mention our second tour in Mattoon and I recall my first fight. A bully about two years older had been stalking me for weeks and finally intercepted me on my way to the store for kerosene. The boy jumped me and I swung. Coincidentally, the same hand I swung with was holding a wire-covered glass gallon jug and it shattered over his head. He ran lickety-split one way, I the other. Somehow he never pestered me again.

Mention Shelbyville, Indiana, and I recall my first pair of roller skates, my first bicycle and my first piano lessons. My interest lasted longer in the skates and bike than it did in the piano.

Mention Owensboro, Kentucky, and I recall buying my first box camera and learning how to develop my own pictures in the cellar. I was finding other learning more difficult—like getting the three "R's" straight in the little red schoolhouse. I was constantly being scolded for staring out the window.

Mention Madison, Indiana, and I recall quitting school for the first time. I went to work in a cotton mill tending a threading machine for $1 a day. Between the racket and the smell, I ended up collecting exactly one dollar.

And so it goes—all typical kid-type memories.

But all through those years I remember the old one-two punch was ever-present: the urges to fish and roam.

I'll never forget the Blue River in Shelbyville where I used to catch plenty of catfish and sunfish. I thought I had pretty good luck until I saw the catfish an old Negro in town would take. Not only did he hook more than I did, but his catches were bigger. To me those 10- and 12-pounders he was taking were monsters.

One day I spotted the old man fishing on the river just in back of where my dad was building a plant. I got up my gumption and asked him his secret.

"Sit right down here, young feller, and watch," he said. "And don't kick over my basket."

Well, sir, that basket was the key to everything. It contained the smelliest, most rotten eggs in the state of Indiana.

"Let me tell you something about Mr. Catfish," the old man said. "He'll go for any food he can get his big mouth around. And the smellier it is the quicker he'll go for it.

"And what smells worse than a rotten egg?" he asked, pointing to his batch that must have been spoiling for weeks.

I had to agree. Boy, I was turning green!

This old fellow knew what he was doing.

He had a very large sproat hook on which he had soldered some light wire to form a pocket for the egg bait. He used a heavy sinker on his line about 18 inches above the hook.

He'd take an egg from the basket, fix it in the pocket around the big hook and puncture each end of the egg with a pin. He'd lower his line gently into the water knowing he wouldn't have long to wait.

In a matter of minutes every catfish in the river got the message. They'd get a whiff of that odor and come running. In no time at all my friend would have himself a prize catch.

And so it went through those years. I fished every chance I got. All I needed was a pole and a can of worms. I was catching mostly catfish and sunfish in whatever state I happened to be in. Heck, I hadn't even heard of a bass or a trout in those days.

And when I wasn't fishing I was wandering.

My folks should have known better than to have ever gotten me a bike. I mean I pedaled that red beauty all over the countryside of wherever we were. I always wondered what was in the next county and would take off to find out—ten, eleven, twelve miles over hill and dale.

The fact that there was no such thing as a paved road didn't bother me. What did was that I invariably caught blazes for these excursions. I'd be gone half the day, miss supper and there would be the devil to pay.

I don't know what I was looking for.

I was like a youngster obsessed.

7. Adventuresville, U.S.A.

ONE FALL NIGHT IN 1909, MY DAD CAME HOME FROM THE GAS plant in Madison.

I helped him stable his horse.

"How would you like to go to Montana, son?" he asked.

"Where?" I gulped.

"Montana," he said. "Great Falls, Montana."

Would I? Would a hungry trout mouth a fat minnow? I almost tore the back door clean off its hinges as I exploded inside to pack my bags.

A month later we headed west by train—the Illinois Central to Chicago, the Great Northern to Great Falls. It was a three-day journey and my nose was glued the entire time to the window of the parlor car dad had reserved for the family. I was enchanted by the ever-changing scene, especially crossing the great plains. It was a delight to my nomad's appetite, and I devoured every morsel.

All the while I was counting the hours to Great Falls. I had great expectations of that central Montana town. And I wasn't disappointed.

I think I could write an entire book on Great Falls as it was at that time. It was a fascinating young city of ten or twelve thousand in those days—a two-fisted boom town of copper smelters carved out of cattle and sheep country.

Every day was an adventure in that town. All I had to do was look out a front window of our company house, and there was the big Missouri River—miles and miles of prime fishing in the summer and mirror-slick ice skating in the winter. And

13

that was just a part of it. Turn any direction in that country and there was something different and exciting to do.

It was just a charming and beautiful land.

Looking back, I can say without a doubt that it was in Great Falls that life began to become really interesting to me.

So many firsts happened to this youngster during the years the family lived there.

It's where I got my first dog . . . my first ice skates . . . my first pony . . . my first rifle . . . my first long pants . . . caught my first rainbow trout . . . made my first hunting trip.

It's where I lived with the Sioux Indians and made my first pack trip into the wilderness and got my first real job.

It's where I met famous people like Buffalo Bill Cody and C. M. Russell.

And it's also where I became really close to my dad.

8.   Father Knew Best

MY DAD WAS THE TYPE OF MAN YOU READ ABOUT IN FICTION: big, strong as an ox, handsome, popular—and reserved until somebody pressed him. Then you'd better batten down the hatches, brother, because all damnation would break loose.

Like I've said, Great Falls is where I came to know dad a whole lot better. I suppose that's natural. When a boy gets into his early teens he and his father can start doing things together.

And, mister, did we ever!

Dad had a hand in just about all the fabulous things that happened to me at Great Falls. A boy couldn't have had a finer father if he could have picked him out of a catalogue. He was a wonderful, wonderful man to his family and knew what made kids tick.

Don't get the idea he was a pal to us. He was a hundred per-cent father and we never forgot who was boss. He was a strict man when he had to be. But usually all he'd have to do was give us kids a look and we'd jump into line.

Once I didn't, though—for the first and last time.

Great Falls had enormous winters. And believe me when I

tell you I saw plenty of 40- and 50-foot snow drifts after three-day blizzards. I made my own sled and would hitch rides behind wagons and buggies. Nobody minded. It wasn't dangerous—not like hooking a coaster onto an automobile or truck today.

Well, sir, I came home around dark one particular afternoon all tuckered out, cold and hungry after a day of coasting. I collapsed on the parlor couch by the big coke burner.

"Vernon, why don't you go out to the shed and get a bucket of coke before supper?" dad said.

"Aw, dad," I said. "I'm too tired."

My father didn't say a word. He just went over and picked up the bucket. I thought he was going to do the chore himself.

"I really got away with that one," I chuckled to myself.

I got away with it, all right—way away.

Dad opened the door and tossed the bucket into the yard. Then he came back, grabbed me off the couch by the scruff of the neck and booted me clear out the door with the side of his foot.

Don't believe all this business about astronauts having been the first men in space. I want to tell you I went into orbit that night.

Somehow I never argued with dad after that. And if I was ever tempted, all I had to do was think back to what happened another night.

When dad came home one particular evening, mom had a message waiting.

"The office called not five minutes ago, George," she said. "There's a bad gas leak or something at one of the saloons."

Dad called the office, and I had a notion there was something wrong by the look on his face. I also knew there had to be some sort of trouble brewing because he could have called one of his crews to fix a gas leak.

"Hold supper, will you, mother?" dad said.

He went to the barn and hitched up the wagon. When dad came back to the house for something, I ducked out the door, snuck into the back of the wagon and covered myself with a horse blanket.

Well, sir, dad drove that wagon like he was in a chariot race clear across to the far edge of town. When he reached the tavern he hopped out—and saw me.

Dad gave me a look, fixed his jaw and ordered: "Stay right where you are, boy. Don't move!"

15

I didn't—until he had swung through the half-doors of that saloon. It was located on a corner, with entrances on two sides. I scrambled out of the wagon and peeked through the opposite door.

And this is what I saw:

The bar was empty except for the saloonkeeper at one end and three rough-looking customers huddled at the other end. Dad marched up to the middle. The barkeeper came over and wiped the counter in front of my father. Inside the cloth was a small nickel-plated pistol.

"Take this, George," he said. "You'll need it."

"Forget it," dad said. "I don't need any gun."

"These boys mean trouble," the saloonkeeper said. "They're the ones stirring up that labor trouble at your gas works."

Dad didn't say a word and strolled to the end of the bar.

"You boys looking for me?" he asked.

Well, sir, those three fellows spread out. It had all the earmarks of a Class B Western.

One roughneck charged and my father side-stepped him. The man bumped up against the bar. That's when dad grabbed him by an arm, jerked the man to him, lifted him and heaved him crashing through a showcase. I can still hear that glass shattering to this day.

A second man made a pass and dad caught him with a lightning right hand that lifted him clear over the bar.

It was an even fight now—one against one—and that last poor devil didn't know whether to stay or run. While he was making up his mind, dad grabbed him by the seat of the britches and pitched him like a sack of oats through the swinging front doors.

And that was that—a saloon brawl that even Hollywood couldn't have topped.

Dad hadn't even broken a sweat, I swear. He walked calmly over to the bartender, thanked him for the use of the hall, and left.

Meanwhile, my eyes as big as saucers, this boy hightailed it back to the wagon. And funny, but dad didn't say a word during the long ride back home—nor did he ever mention that fight to me as long as he lived.

Well, sir, that was the kind of dad I had.

It might sound kind of funny after what happened in that saloon, but my father was an enormously popular man. He really was. He knew everyone around town.

One of his very good friends was C. M. Russell, the great cowboy artist. I spent many an hour at Charley's house listening to his stories of prairie life and watching him bring them to life magically on canvas. I'd be glued to the chair.

There's a sort of sad, bang-your-head-against-the-wall type postscript to the friendship of my dad and C. M. Russell.

He had given my father two of his originals back in Great Falls. And, as such things happen, they got shunted to the attic over the years as my folks moved from town to town. I guess we all pretty much forgot about them. Besides, Russell's popularity wasn't what it became years later.

Well, not too many years ago one of the big magazines did a big spread on Charley and told how one of his major works couldn't be found. It estimated its current value at about $250,000.

I nearly keeled over because the description pretty much fitted that of one of two pictures Russell had given dad.

My sisters did some detective work and the search ended at Lillian's house. When mother had died, Lillian had cleaned out of the attic a lot of old trunks and pictures. She figured they were just dust-catchers and burned them.

So we'll never know if we had the quarter-million-dollar beauty. The answer went up in smoke.

Another man dad knew was none other than William F. Cody, old "Buffalo Bill."

That great American plainsman and scout came to Great Falls once as advance man for his famous wild west show that was due to hit town the next day.

My father came home for dinner early that night.

"I'm taking you back into town after supper," he told me. "There's a man I want you to meet."

Naturally I began pressing him as to who the man was.

"Just a man I used to know years ago," he said.

We headed into town and dad pulled the wagon up in front of a saloon.

"Oh, oh," I said to myself. "Here we go again!"

But I knew it would be different. For one thing, dad invited me in. For another, this was the old Silver Dollar Saloon—billed as having "the longest bar west of Chicago." Imbedded right in the floor were real silver dollars spelling out the words "Silver Dollar" in big thick letters.

And there standing at the bar was Buffalo Bill in glistening

17

buckskin. He was in his sixties then, but still was a handsome man with a well-manicured silver beard.

"I hear you're quite a rider, boy," Mr. Cody said.

I guess I blushed a bit.

"I'll find out tomorrow," he said. "You'll ride with me in the welcoming parade."

And I did.

I rode as an escort for Buffalo Bill and at one point in the parade he even switched horses with me. It was a tremendous thrill.

But I'm getting away from my story here and putting the horse before the pony. I haven't told yet about my first pony—a pinto beauty.

A tribe of Sioux Indians camped across the river from Great Falls in those days. There must have been five hundred of them and they were led by Chief Little Bear, a one-time protégé of Sitting Bull. He's the boy who had done in General Custer thirty-five years before at Little Bighorn, not more than a couple of hundred miles across the Wyoming border from where we were.

The Sioux caught wild horses, broke them and sold them. And my father bought plenty for his work. So he got to know these boys pretty well, especially Little Bear.

One day dad was picking out a couple of horses at the camp and I must have had a special look of envy in my face.

"Okay, Vernon," he said. "Which one do you want for your own?"

I was paralyzed with delight.

I chose a handsome bay and white spotted colt.

The Chief shook his head. He explained that this pinto hadn't even been ridden yet and that I should pick another. Then it was my turn to shake my head. I didn't care if that critter was trained or not. I *had* to have him.

Little Bear figured he'd fix that. He sent out a brave—that's when I learned why they were called braves—to ride the pony.

Talk about a job of bucking! That young horse threw that poor Sioux three or four times. The Indian came back grumbling and shaking his head.

"See?" said Little Bear smugly.

"I've got to have him, Chief," I pleaded.

My father threw up his hands.

I wouldn't be surprised if dad had a little glint in his eye at the same time. It's just possible he saw a little of himself in me. Dad loved horses and had always kept two or three no matter where we traveled. He had them as much for sport as for transportation. And it seemed the wilder the better. I remember one he'd had a few years back in Mattoon. There was a colt nobody could bust. Dad bought him, broke him to harness—and had him winning on the Illinois trotting circuit within a year.

Well, sir, Little Bear, dad and myself were still kicking around my problem of the pony. The big worry was that even if we could get that pony back home somehow, he could be a danger in the neighborhood. Besides, I just might end up getting killed.

It was the Chief who finally came up with a solution. He suggested I come back to his camp every weekend until the pinto could be broken. I could live right with the tribe.

This was *too* good to be true.

And believe me or not, my father agreed to it. He was that friendly with Little Bear and trusted him completely. Dad paid the Chief $15 for my pony and we headed home across the river. And if you think this lad slept a wink until the next weekend, you're fooling yourself.

To shorten a long story, I lived with those Sioux for about three weekends. I slept in their teepees, ate their food, lent a hand in caring for their horses—and helped them break my pony. Or tried to.

That pinto—and I named him "Pinto"—spent those three weekends pitching me all over the prairie. I had a bridle on him, but no saddle—another sore point. He'd get up a head of steam and, square in the middle of a dead gallop, execute what I swear was a 90-degree turn. The trouble was I'd keep sailing straight ahead.

We finally busted that animal. Those Indians knew how to ride a horse and taught me well. I got so I could do all sorts of tricks with him—get on and off on the dead gallop, ride him backwards, the whole works.

Boy, I loved that pony. Dad bought me a saddle and I rode that horse constantly the next three years. Talk about Mary and her little lamb! Pinto and I did everything together—even fished. In fact that colt even helped me land my first trout.

Dad would take his men on outings about once a month during the summer. These men were mostly immigrants from Europe. They worked hard and my father wanted to make

19

sure they kept much of what they earned by keeping them out of gambling halls as much as he could.

He'd load several kegs of beer and a pile of ice on one wagon, the boys in four or five others, and head up to the Great Falls about seven miles out of town and camp for the day. The boys would have themselves quite a time.

The first time I was allowed to go along I ran true to form and wandered. Just above the Great Falls, I discovered Horseshoe Falls. I curled up on shore at the foot of the falls and observed some fish I'd never seen before. They were a beautiful fish—red striped and black dotted—and looked to weigh an average of about four pounds.

I had been fishing for carp in the Missouri from just about the day I'd arrived in Montana. I'd become quite successful catching them on dough balls, as I wandered up and down that river.

So I looked at these rainbows and itched. Man, did I want to fish those beauties. I didn't have any gear along but made up my mind to come back the next chance I had. And within a week I was back—aboard Pinto and as excited as a robin in a fresh-plowed garden.

Never mind a snap or a swivel or a leader or those fancy gadgets. I had an extra-long cane pole—it must have been 14 feet—along with some regular chalk line, a small sinker and a big hook which must have been a No. 2, although I didn't know anything about sizes in those days. For bait I caught a bunch of big yellow grasshoppers right along shore.

No sooner had I put the line into the water than I nearly lost it. I'd hooked an enormous rainbow—at least six or seven pounds. And he was doing tricks I'd never seen before on the end of any line. Let me tell you, friend, a cane pole is no fly rod. But somehow I horsed that old rainbow onto the bank and had the prize of my life. I can't describe the thrill.

In no time at all, I caught three or four more. Finally, though, I hooked one whose number I *didn't* have. He splintered my pole clean down the middle. For all I know, there's a granddaddy trout still swimming the Missouri carrying half a length of bamboo pole on his back.

I paraded home that night as proud as a peacock in courting season.

I thought I was an honest-to-goodness trout fisherman.

Little did I know I was about to become something else: a hunter.

9. The Great Education

DAD NEVER CARED MUCH FOR FISHING. BUT HOW THAT MAN loved to hunt!

It seems he was always heading for the boondocks with a rifle over his shoulder as far back as I can remember. He had a passion for shooting any kind of game: deer, bear, quail— you name it. And let me tell you, mister, he was an expert.

I had always been after him to take me with him. But it was always the same old refrain: "Not yet, son. You're too young. One of these days I'll surprise you."

"One of these days" turned out to be my fourteenth birthday—January 28, 1910. Dad presented me with a spanking-new single-shot .22 rifle and I *was* surprised—and delighted.

My father spent the rest of the winter checking me out on the weapon. He was not only a crackajack hunter, but a safe one. And he wanted to make sure I was too.

When spring finally arrived, dad took me to the flat lands outside of town and showed me how to shoot prairie chickens, which we took home to eat.

Soon after, an inseparable buddy named Tom Clayton and I found a hunting spot even closer. It was a little island in the Missouri just west of town. We'd wade out to that patch of paradise and be in a world of our own. It was loaded with rabbits and I would get some good practice with my .22 and have some game to take home as well.

It wasn't long before I was going for a lot bigger game.

"C'mon, son, get packed up," dad said one Friday night that fall. "We're going to do some hunting—some *real* hunting.

"And saddle up real good. We'll be gone a week."

Our destination: the foothills of the Rocky Mountains.

The next morning dad, two of his top men and I took the train from Great Falls about 100 miles south to Belt, Montana. From there we took a stagecoach to a little copper-mining town called Neihart, where we spent the night with some miners in a dormitory-style building.

The next day a guide named Williams—he was an old friend of my father's—took us by horseback a half-dozen

21

miles or so farther into the wilderness to a little abandoned camp. The government had built it years before for workers during a tremendous forest fire in that neck of the woods. There were a couple of cabins there, and dad and I shared one.

My father's whispers woke me the next morning.

"Vernon!" he buzzed. "Psst, Vernon!"

He was standing by the door with his rifle and I scrambled over to join him.

Not fifty yards away was a big old black bear sniffing around a spring. It took dad one shot to drop him.

Well, sir, that whole area was crawling with deer as well as bear, and in three days dad had his three-deer limit. All the while I was learning. My father wouldn't let me shoot at the deer, just watch. After he'd bag his deer for the day, he'd let me pick off a fool hen sprucegrouse or two on our way back to camp.

On Saturday we returned to Neihart despite one of the heaviest snowstorms I've ever seen. We only had to go about six miles, but it seemed half a continent. We'd never have made it without some of the most sure-footed horses in captivity. The next day—boy, it was bitter cold—we grabbed the stage to Belt where we caught the train to Great Falls.

It had been a fabulous, fabulous trip. And, content on a bellyful of venison and the knowledge my dad now considered me a man, I slept all the way home on that bumpy day coach.

What I didn't know was that this expedition had been part of a schedule that dad had carefully plotted to educate me as a complete hunter. Graduation would come the day he could take me on one of his annual two-week trips higher into the Rockies.

There was one more trial I had to pass—the most wonderful test a boy ever faced: a six-week pack trip.

My father employed an old man named Tom Church as a sort of general handyman. Now here was a marvelous character—one of the last of the mountaineers, a man well into his seventies who still rode tall in the saddle. Old Tom didn't need the money—he had fat bank accounts in both Great Falls and Helena. But he wanted to keep active and not shrivel up in a corner somewhere just because he was past sixty-five.

I loved that man, I really did. He'd keep me spellbound for hours with his stories of fighting the Indians, trapping in the

22

mountains and carving out a living on the frontier. He had done everything and I wanted to be just like him.

One day the next summer Tom came to me and said, "Get packed, boy. We're taking a trip."

And did we ever!

For six weeks we traipsed all around southern Montana and northern Wyoming and Idaho on horseback—all through Yellowstone country. Today a lot of that area is part of the National Park. But fifty years ago it was wilderness. All the while we lived by old Tom's wit and pluck. We had taken some supplies along, but lived mostly off the land.

And, brother, I learned.

Tom taught me how to read signs, where to find good water and how to build shelter out of practically nothing. He taught me how to build fires—and how to put them out. He taught me how to care for our horses and four pack animals. He taught me how to trap, hunt and fish. He taught me how to eat everything from grouse to snake. And he taught me a million and one other things.

I was always asking questions and the old man had all the answers.

It was a fabulous, fabulous education—one that boys even in that time didn't often get. It was an opportunity of a lifetime and I'm still reaping the benefits of it more than fifty-five years later.

It had more immediate benefits too. That fall my father took me up into the Rockies with him.

Don't get the idea my education in Great Falls was all of the outdoor variety. I also learned a lot about everyday life.

Not in a classroom though.

I quit school after finishing the eighth grade in 1910. Education wasn't what it is today. A grammar school diploma was pretty much what a high school diploma is today. Still, my quitting upset my folks, who had wanted me to go a lot further. I always felt dad would have liked me to be an engineer. They had let out a sigh of relief when I'd returned to school after quitting for those few days in Madison. Now they knew I hadn't learned from it.

I hated disappointing my parents, but I had to. I thought I was learning more about life outside the schoolhouse than I could inside. In later years I realized how wrong I had been.

My father didn't fret about it too long. He just put me to work for the gas company. First I was assigned to bring water

23

to the men working in the ditches as the company dug mile upon mile for the gas main all around town. Then I graduated into some pick and shovel work myself. And later I even did a little dynamiting.

It was quite an experience working with those men. They were tough *hombres*. I recall when one of them had a little too much to drink one sweltering day, leaped out of the trench and attacked my father with a knife. Dad picked up a pick handle and broke the fellow's arm with one swing.

After six months I found a way to earn a lot more money with a lot less sweat. A hotel had just been built in town—a fabulous place with an all-marble lobby and winding staircase —and I got a job as bellboy.

Talk about an education!

Between the dance hall and gambling rooms, that hotel jumped till all hours with miners and cattlemen who had money burning holes in their pockets. Cash was free and easy, and I was making $100 a month with no trouble—pretty good money for a fifteen-year-old.

Yes, sir, I was getting to be a big shot all right.

I knew Buffalo Bill Cody, didn't I? C. M. Russell too. And gamblers and dancing girls.

I was a man all right, I thought.

The year before my father had bought me my first pair of long pants. No more knickers for me. Dad brought me to a tailor shop and had a grey flannel suit made for me for $12. And if you can believe it, I went out the next day and bought me a pair of purple socks and tan shoes with some money I'd earned.

I thought I was the cat's whiskers.

What my father had been dolling me up for was another of the priceless moments of my life—the legendary Jim Jeffries-Jack Johnson world heavyweight championship fight at Reno on July 4, 1910.

We traveled to Nevada by train and were among the sixteen thousand who crowded into Reno's open air arena. From what we'd read in the press, we knew it was going to be a controversial fight. Any doubt was erased as we entered the arena. We were searched. Police checked all firearms at the gate and issued receipts. Everyone carried pistols in that country in those days; by opening bell the police had accumulated a small arsenal.

An hour or so later I was happy they had. Johnson knocked out Jeffries in fifteen rounds to ignite all sorts of riots—and all around the country in fact when word of the outcome got out by wireless.

Yes, sir, I got quite an education during my years in Great Falls—a priceless education.

Yet it was only the beginning.

Next stop: the Ohio River.

10. *My First Bass*

I DIDN'T GO TO THE OHIO. THE OHIO CAME TO ME.

I mean that river came pouring into our living room four feet deep.

The Gaddis family, with its wonder knack of timing, had moved to Paducah, Kentucky, just in time for the big 1913 flood that killed nearly a thousand people from Ohio to Missouri.

I could have landed a sunfish under the dining room table.

That flood ruined a lot of people in Paducah. But Paducah ruined me for another reason.

It's the town where I caught my first crappie, then my first bass. And once I hooked that first bass, I was a goner. I couldn't have quit fishing after that if my life had depended on it.

I didn't get a crack at those fish right off. I was delayed about one full year from our arrival in town. My family had left Great Falls just before Christmas and had detoured by Mattoon to spend the holidays with all the relations at the old homestead. We had arrived in Paducah sometime in January and were just getting settled when the big flood hit in late March.

That flood left the whole area unsettled until midsummer. And by that time, I had myself a job. I worked for dad cleaning gas lamps in all the business houses, department stores and hotels downtown. I'd go around with a ladder cleaning and adjusting the lights so they'd burn bright.

Meanwhile, I took to hanging around a place called Clemens Book Store. It actually carried a lot more sporting goods than books. Harry Clemens was a fine man and an excellent fisherman. A lot of the anglers in town hung around his place, and I was in there every chance I got. I was thinking about fishing more than I ever had in my life.

All winter long we sat around an old pot-belly stove and talked fishing. And all I heard was stories about the slews across the Ohio River on the Illinois shore and all the fat bass and crappie that could be taken there in the spring.

"When it warms up, son, I'll take you fishing over there," Harry would tell me. "These fish are something you just have to see to believe."

I could believe them, all right. That's all I'd been hearing for months. That winter seemed an eternity, the longest of my life. I never thought it would pass. Meanwhile, I saved my money and bought a reel, rod, line and some old Wilson wobbler plugs. I passed the hours shining that gear till I had what must have been the most lustrous tackle in the state of Kentucky.

Spring finally broke and I was there to greet it. A shoemaker in town was a real fishing buff, and one noon he said to me at the book store, "Tomorrow's the day, Vernon. We'll leave from my shop at daybreak."

I didn't want to take any chances. I got permission to sleep right in the shoemaker's shop all night. I'll never forget lying on that cobbler's bench all night and not sleeping a wink because I was so excited.

Come daylight, and the shoemaker didn't have to call me. I was waiting on him. We hopped into his boat at the wharf and rowed across the river to a sandbar on the Illinois side. We seined off the bar and came up with more than enough live bait to fill our buckets.

It wasn't far from there into the slews and bass and crappie country. And it wasn't long before we had plenty of 1- to 1½-pound crappie—good-size catches.

We didn't hook any bass, but I wasn't too disappointed. These were my first crappie, and I'd gotten a thrill out of catching them. Besides, I knew tomorrow was another day.

And was it ever!

Harry Clemens had wanted me to wait for the weekend so he could take me over. I couldn't wait. I borrowed a boat—a leaky one, at that, which I was constantly bailing out—and headed across the Ohio into Illinois by myself.

Casting was new to me and I had some trouble with it. But I unsnarled the backlashes and learned from it. I wasn't too expert at fishing the plugs I was using either.

But somehow I had a tremendous strike. A 4- or 5-pound bass hit my plug, and that old boy didn't have a chance.

I was so excited I stood up in the boat and started reeling in that poor fish across the water on the ride of his life. It's a wonder I didn't break the line and lose him—or lose myself overboard.

I hauled that bass into the boat, shoved him under the bow and stuffed my coat in behind him like I thought he was going to fly away or something. Then I turned around and rowed like the dickens home so I could show that prize to my mother.

Boy, was I excited! And was I hooked!

I was a goner on bass fishing for life.

I was fascinated by those creatures. I'd lie on a log along a slew for hours on a Saturday or Sunday and study these fish. The water was clear and I tried to analyze their every move. I wanted to know all about these customers. I'd have a friend cast a plug near the bass and watch their reaction to it.

I watched that pugnacious cuss smack at the plug one time, ignore it the next. If nothing else, I learned that no one in the world knows what's going on in the mind of that bass.

Meanwhile, I kept after my bait casting. I went fishing every chance I got—before work, after work, weekends. And sometimes I'd play hooky. Mr. Clemens and some of the boys from his hot stove league would come along and help me plenty. In no time I became a fair-to-middlin' bass fisherman.

And it got so people would ask me to take them along. I was happy to because I love company.

There was one man I wished I'd left home though: a wonderful gentleman by the name of Cohen.

Mr. Cohen was chief engineer at the power plant. He was very hard of hearing—probably from spending his life in those deafening power plants. He was also a little forgetful.

One day I took Mr. Cohen and a friend of his into the slews. We weren't having too much luck at one particular spot and the two men were getting itchy to try another area.

"Go ahead," I said. "I'm going to stay here for awhile. I

27

know there are a couple of bass here and I'm going to out-wait them."

I outwaited them all right. I also outwaited my friends.

Believe it or not, they forgot about me completely. They got so excited over a couple of catches that they took off for home, leaving me stranded on the other side of the river.

That didn't disturb me. It really didn't. Maybe it was the adventure of it. It was getting dark so I gathered some wood, built a fire, made a bed out of dry leaves and prepared to spend the night.

Even one heck of a thunder and lightning storm—it clattered to beat the band—didn't shake me up. I got plenty wet, but that didn't bother me.

What I didn't know was that there was also some thundering and lightning of another sort going on back in Paducah. My mother had begun worrying when I didn't get home before the storm and called Mr. Cohen.

"Oh my gosh!" he said. "We got so excited about a couple of bass we plumb forgot him!"

I guess mom let him have it pretty good.

Well, sir, about midnight I saw some lanterns coming across the levee and heard some calls.

It was Mr. Cohen and his friend.

"Forget something, boys?" I needled.

I thought Mr. Cohen was going to have a stroke apologizing. He didn't have to though. He had the best excuse anyone could ever have.

I never blame a man for getting a little excited over some plump bass.

11. A Man Named Cobb

ONE MORNING THE DOORBELL CHIMED.

"Is Vern home?" a heavyset man asked.

My mother fetched me.

"I understand you know where to catch the best live bait in town," the man said to me. "Will you get me some?"

I did and the man came back several times. Each time he gave me a dollar, an awful lot of money to a kid like me. The third time he asked me to go fishing with him.

He was about forty and seemed an extremely pleasant gentleman. I figured I just might enjoy his company, so I accepted.

"My name is Cobb—Irvin Cobb," he said, and we shook hands.

The name didn't make an impression on me. Even if I'd been given his full monicker—Irvin S. Cobb—I still wouldn't have known that this Paducah native was world famous as one of the great American humorists of our time.

To me he was just Mr. Cobb, a man with a yen for bass and crappie fishing. For all I cared he might have been Joe Doakes —which I'm sure is exactly the way Mr. Cobb preferred it. He was a simple, easy-going man without any airs.

Well, sir, we hit it off right from the start. Here was a wonderful man who could put a youngster in a spell.

We'd sit along the slews across the Ohio River and fish and gab half the day. Mr. Cobb was a man with a lot of intelligence and a lot of wit. What he said made sense in a wonderful sort of way.

What really captivated me was his knowledge of steamboats.

He loved steamboats and I loved steamboats.

We'd see one plowing by on the Ohio on its way to the Mississippi a few miles west at Cairo and that would start me asking all sorts of questions. And Mr. Cobb had all the answers.

He knew what made steamers tick and he knew the lore of the Mississippi. He could really spin a story, and I'd listen to him for hours.

Mississippi riverboats were in high fashion as passenger, gambling and cargo vessels in the middle 1800s. The ports deteriorated somewhat after the Civil War as railroads began springing up like wild flowers. Yet river life had continued to be heavy if not vital, and I was intrigued by it.

And nothing captivated me more than the showboats. There was something. What I wouldn't give to see one today!

Everybody loved the showboat. Posters would be tacked up all over town in advance of its coming, and the whole town would turn out for its arrival.

And when that old boat turned the bend, its calliopes whistling, everyone went wild. As soon as she docked there'd be a parade around town with the show people. And you can guess who'd always be right in the middle. I mean I just couldn't get enough of it. It was really something—a wonderful, wonderful flavor of everybody loving everybody that's sadly lacking in America today.

And to me this was the part of the Mississippi riverboating that entranced me so.

Mr. Cobb knew it all and I sponged up his every word.

I can't recall all our palaver word for word, of course. But I do remember one conversation crystal clear.

"What are you going to be when you grow up, Vern?" Mr. Cobb asked one afternoon.

"A steamboat pilot," I answered matter-of-factly.

And that was that.

12. Two Strikes—I'm Out

WHEN I WASN'T FISHING, I PLAYED BASEBALL EVERY CHANCE I got.

And if you want to get me bragging, brother, just ask me what kind of ball player I was. Even if you don't, I'll tell you right out: I thought I was pretty darn good. I was a line-drive hitter, a fast runner and could field my position at third base.

At least one other man thought so too, a wonderful gentleman named William E. Potter. And because he did, I had a chance at tryouts with two major league teams.

Who knows today I might have been Vern Gaddis the former Chicago White Soxer or St. Louis Cardinal instead of Gadabout Gaddis The Flying Fisherman.

That I'm not isn't any fault of Mr. Potter.

My father worked with Mr. Potter. Mr. Potter bought the locations and dad built gas houses on them. Mr. Potter was a big man around Chicago and knew all the baseball people, including White Sox owner Charles A. Comiskey.

Mr. Potter saw me play plenty of sandlot ball around Paducah.

"Vern," he said one spring day in 1915, "how would you like to come up to Chicago and meet Mr. Comiskey and his White Sox?

"They just might be interested in a ball player like you."

Well, sir, you can imagine the dreams that started swimming around in my head.

Paducah had a team in the Kitty League then which I often went to see. I thought it had great players and imitated their every move.

Now I was going to see—and meet—the big league Chicago White Sox!

The White Sox had become an exciting team that season. They were to become world champions in 1917 before falling into disgrace as the Black Sox of 1919.

But in 1915 they were the talk of baseball as an up-and-coming team that had just added the great Eddie Collins and Shoeless Joe Jackson to go along with such stars as Red Faber, Ed Cicotte and Ray Schalk.

I met Mr. Potter in Chicago the next week. My train was a couple of hours late and he took me directly to Comiskey Park.

It was located exactly where it is now, on the corner of 35th Street and Shields Avenue on the South Side. The park was about five years old at the time and enough to take a nineteen-year-old prairie boy's breath away. It was only single-decked then, but was the biggest, most beautiful darn ball yard this rube had ever seen.

Mr. Potter knew those baseball people *real* good. Inside fifteen minutes I was rubbing elbows in the dugout with all the big names I'd read about.

Outside of meeting Rube Marquard, the great New York Giants pitcher, a year or so before when he'd passed through Paducah, these were the first big leaguers I'd ever seen.

Finally Mr. Potter introduced me to the Chicago manager, Clarence (Pants) Rowland.

"I hear you're quite a ball player," he said.

I was so shook I don't know what I replied, if anything.

"Look, son," he said. "I want to give you a look. But it's going to have to wait awhile. We don't have enough time before today's game. And right afterwards we're catching a train East. The club will be back in town in a couple of weeks and I want you to come back then, okay?"

I was disappointed but not crushed. At least I could watch the game that day. And I did.

Funny, I can't recall who the White Sox played or who won. But I do remember that of all the big-name heroes on the field, the player who caught my fancy was a fellow named Buck Weaver. He was only a .270 or so hitter, but was a marvel covering the left side of the infield. I couldn't take my eyes off him.

I wondered how I was going to take his job away.

Mr. Potter was probably even more disappointed about my missing a tryout than I was. But he was a persistent man and not about to be discouraged so easily.

"You go ahead home, Vern," he told me the next day. "You'll be hearing from me."

I did, two weeks later. He wrote that he had set up a tryout for the following week with manager Miller Huggins of the Cardinals in St. Louis. And there would be no slipup this time because the Cards would be starting a long homestand.

So I packed up again, said my goodbyes and headed for St. Louis.

An odd thing happened when I got there.

I had purposely arrived a day early to nose around the city while the team was still on the road. But something got into me in the next few hours.

Maybe it was because the Cardinals were a lackluster second-division team. Maybe it was because the idea of a try-out was anticlimactic after the White Sox episode. Or just maybe it was because I heard bass were running thick and fast in the White River.

Whatever the reason, I took off and fished that White River for a week in Arkansas.

Don't ask me why.

Lord knows my dad did. So did Mr. Potter. But I couldn't explain it to them then any more than I can to you today.

It had been an impulsive thing. And to this day I have some minor regrets about it.

It's not that I would have preferred to have been a ball player. It's just that I'll always wonder if I could have made the grade.

There's no telling what might have come out of that tryout. And that's just the point. So from time to time I still catch myself mulling what might have been.

In some ways I think I might have been able to make a go in baseball. But, then again, I probably wouldn't have.

To be good in anything a man has to love it and concentrate on it.

And I obviously was more interested in just one thing: fishing.

13. My First Trip

THAT TRIP ON THE WHITE RIVER RUINED ME.

It had been like teasing a frisky kitten with a sniff of catnip. I craved more.

My feet were itchy in Paducah and I became restless.

No longer was I content to see what was in the next town or the next county. Nor even the next state. I wanted to see what was in the state after that and beyond.

Meanwhile, I was working on a number of jobs. I was still with the gas company. I was squeezing in a little apprenticing as a pipe fitter on the side. And nights I was working as an usher and stage hand at the Paducah Opera House—ushering for picture shows like *Birth of a Nation* (which, I'll never forget, carried its own orchestra), propping for all the stage shows.

Some of the work was interesting—especially show business, which I loved.

Still—and I can't really explain it—I was bored. I yearned to travel on my own.

By early fall I couldn't contain my fiddle-feet any longer.

A pal named Fred James and I plotted the expedition.

I told my parents about it, of course. They didn't like it, but didn't try to stop me. They knew restlessness was tearing out my insides.

So one night Fred and I hopped a freight bound for Memphis.

We had exactly $3 apiece and were off on the trip of our lives.

14. Beggars Can Be Choosers

A MAN CAN BUM AROUND THE COUNTRY WITHOUT BEING A bum.

You are not a tramp unless you feel or act like one.

I often traveled for days as a young fellow with less than a dime in my pocket. But I never lost my pride or self-respect. There wasn't any need to. I could keep my head high by simply using it. A person can get along merely by using the brains his Creator gave him.

Let's get a couple of matters clear from the start.

What I'm going to be talking about here not only concerns my first trip in 1915 with my chum Fred. It also goes for the many, many more trips I took by myself clear through the middle 1920s. The reason I'm lumping it all together is simple. My approach to the fine art of going where I wanted on practically nothing was always the same during all of my ramblings.

Also, I don't want anyone—especially youngsters—to read this and get the idea that I'm saying this can be done today. I'm not. I did it more than forty and fifty years ago. Times and laws have changed. So I'm not recommending that anyone try what I did. I'm just telling of my experiences as I try to explain the jigsaw that's been my life.

There are three necessities for a man on the move. He needs transportation, something in his belly and a place to lay his head.

I never had trouble lining up any one of them as I followed the birds.

Transportation was easy.

If I was broke I'd hop a freight train. I'd had a head start in knowing how to ride the rails successfully. A couple of my uncles were railroad men and had taken me on the Mattoon-to-Evansville run two or three times. I learned a lot about how a railroad operated by listening to them.

That's why I usually never hopped a boxcar blind. I went about it with a plan and knew a freight's destination before I boarded it.

34

I'd go to the yardmaster's office and check the big manifest blackboards which listed all traffic by train, track, time, destination and conductor.

I'd pick the train I wanted and climb aboard the caboose just before departure time. There I'd find the conductor whose name I'd have gotten from the manifest.

Almost invariably, this would be the conversation:

"What do you want, son?"

"Mr. Jones, my name is Vern Gaddis. My uncle works for the railroad. Maybe you know him: Doll Prince? Anyway, I have to get to such-and-such place for such-and-such reason. Can you help me out?"

Nine times out of ten the conductor would point out a boxcar.

"Go in there," he'd say. "No one will bother you."

So it was seldom I had trouble getting rides.

Oh, there were times I'd have to catch a train without permission for one reason or another. But that was rare. And I made sure it was rare for at least three very good reasons.

One was that hopping a train was against the law. You could be slapped into jail for it. At the very least you'd be booted off at the first opportunity. And you were in serious trouble if you got kicked off a train.

More often than not you'd be bounced into the middle of nowhere. It would be a long, long walk to somewhere. And it could be even tougher if you were thrown off in a little town. Big cities swallow up strangers. But everybody knows everybody in little towns and they didn't like strangers in those days. They considered you a vagrant and made it tough.

So I was always scared stiff I'd be kicked off, but I never was—mostly because I took the precaution of checking first with the conductor.

Once I didn't, though, near the end of my very first trip.

Fred and I did the silliest thing in the world. We blinded a passenger train bound for Kansas City. "Blinding" is riding the blinders in the back of the engine.

We like to froze to death. And it was the dirtiest trip of my life as well as the coldest. It was a nightmare.

Chalk it up to inexperience. I never did it again.

I learned other things too—like what kind of boxcar to avoid.

A car filled with lumber is plain suicide. If that engine hits the brakes fast, the lumber will shift and pin a man in.

Or it will scatter like tenpins and clobber everything and everybody in its way. Either way, you've had it.

A car loaded with watermelon or cotton seed is no picnic either. I slept on top of melons one night and was sore for a week. I tucked myself in among cotton another night and itched for *two* weeks.

So I lived and learned.

I also stuck by another rule which helped keep me safe.

I never rode in a boxcar with a stranger. If I found it occupied, I'd move to another. If none were empty, I'd wait for another train. It wasn't that I was being too choosy. It's just that I never wanted to be locked up in a speeding car with a man who might turn out to be desperate or a little off his rocker. I'd heard of cases like that and made up my mind never to get caught in that kind of a fix. And I never did.

I found freights the best way to travel. Not only couldn't you beat the price, but they were fast and safe.

In all the thousands upon thousands of miles I rode on those trains—on wood, as well as coal-burners—I was in only one accident. And, funny, that came when I was on a joyride up front as a guest of the engineer.

That happened on my first trip too. Fred and I were staying a week in Jonesboro, Arkansas, and I became friendly with an engineer on the Jonesboro, Lake City and Eastern Railroad—the old J.L.C.&E.

The entire length of that railroad was only about sixty miles. One day the engineer asked if I'd like to make the trip. I did, and on the way back that doggone train jumped the track. Luckily no one was hurt.

Other than that, I never got a scratch.

Yes, sir, I'll always have a good word for the railroad.

A place to sleep was no problem in my travels either.

If worse came to worse, I'd just curl up close to a railroad water tower or under a tree somewhere. It does a man good to sleep under the stars now and then.

If it was too cool for that, I'd simply walk into the local jail and tell the sheriff I needed a place to lay my head for the night. He'd put me up. I did that plenty of times, although many a lockup I walked right out of again because it was so filthy.

A place I'd never go for the night was to one of those hobo camps along the tracks. They were bad news. Many of these

36

men had lost their self-respect and it was truly a survival of the fittest in their jungles.

I remember one night near Marktree, Arkansas, I made the mistake of sleeping too close to one of these camps, about a mile up the tracks. During the night I awoke with a start. A bearded old man was trying to take the shoes right off my feet. I jumped up and stared at him blurry-eyed.

"Sorry," he shrugged. "They looked like a good pair of shoes. I thought I could use them. You can't blame a man for trying."

So I stayed clear of those boys.

I was very fortunate. I sure met some characters. But I never ran into any jams.

Getting a meal was no sweat either.

If there was no other way, I'd find the finest restaurant in town and ask for the manager. I'd level with him—identify myself (I never faked a name), say that I was a stranger in town looking for a job, tell him I was hungry, and ask if there was anything I could do to get something to eat.

I used this approach for two reasons. One was that I wanted to go first class even if I couldn't afford it. Don't let anyone fool you: beggars *can* be choosers. The other reason was that it was actually the easiest way to get fed in those days.

Usually the manager would say: "Sit down, son. We'll fix you right up." And when I had finished, he'd say: "Okay, young fellow. Hope you enjoyed it. See you later."

Nine times out of ten they wouldn't ask for anything in return. Rarely, they might ask me to sweep out the place or some such minor chore. But, believe it or not, I never was asked to wash a single dish.

I used this procedure often. I'm not talking about just in hick towns. I did it plenty in such cities as St. Louis, Houston and San Francisco.

I got by with this approach for a couple of reasons.

One was that I picked my spots. Professional hoboes always picked eateries near the railroad tracks to try to mooch a meal. Those proprietors were used to them and would slam the door in their faces.

I picked the fancy places where they weren't used to having people approach them without money.

Also, I might have been broke. But I never looked like a bum.

I wore a clean suit under my jacket-and-overalls traveling

37

togs. I carried a razor kit and would freshen up as best I could in the railroad yards when I hit a town.

Then I'd head downtown to a hotel. There were very few private baths in those days and I'd walk directly up to the second or third floor washroom. I looked like any other guest and would ask a maid for a towel and soap. Then I'd bolt the door and bathe, put on a closer shave and get all spruced up. No trouble.

I often got a few hours' sleep in an honest-to-goodness bed in these hotels too. After getting scrubbed up, I'd see the maid in the corridor and tell her how I'd been up all night and was a little short on cash. Usually she'd point out an empty room where I could rest for forty winks. What's more, she'd come back and wake me when her tour was over so I could get on my way—to a first-class restaurant pronto.

So getting a meal in a big city was no problem. Neither was it in the middle of nowhere.

I'd just find a farm and ask what I could do to earn something to eat. Usually the farmer would fill my belly for merely splitting a little wood. And almost always his wife would pack me a lunch for the road too.

There's a moral here, don't you see? It's simply that people are basically kind and helpful. All you have to do is be honest with them and they'll do anything in the world for you. It's human nature. Just don't try to con them. If nothing else during my travels, I learned this lesson of faith in my fellow man. And I've never forgotten it.

I can cite example after example: the conductor, the restaurant manager, the maid, the farmer. And there were many, many others.

I can remember freezing by a railroad siding one night somewhere in the South. The night watchman from a nearby sawmill came by. He took me inside to sleep in the boiler room for the night.

"It ain't much, son," he almost apologized. "But it's warm."

I can recall many a night shivering near shack-sized depots on lonely western prairies. The telegrapher would spot me and invite me in until the train came through. These kindly men would help in any way they could—often going so far as to get permission from the engineer to get you aboard the train.

I can't see a Western today without thinking of the many hours I spent in these tiny depots gabbing with the operators and listening to the ticker clattering messages in and out.

38

So it doesn't matter about human nature. It's the same north, south, east and west—all basically marvelous.

Now I've been dwelling on the many times I grubbed our room, board and transportation. But more often I paid my own way. I did it by earning money.

Don't let anyone ever tell you that a body can't pick up a couple of quick, honest dollars if he wants them badly enough. All he has to do is work for them. And I worked in most every job imaginable.

I was a handyman in a Baptist church in Arkansas, a gandy dancer on a railroad gang in Iowa, a newsboy in California, a concrete mixer on a construction crew in Nebraska, a plumber's helper in Arizona and a vacuum cleaner salesman in Minnesota. I drove a hard-tailed mule team in Louisiana and milked cows in Wisconsin. I was a logger in Oregon and a gold miner in Colorado.

And these are only a few of the jobs I had. I could go on and on. What I did was a little bit of everything. If a job showed up, I'd do it. I'd work at it two or three weeks and make enough money to keep moving on.

A man could stretch $15 or $20 a long way.

My ace in the hole was selling newspapers or magazines. That's why I never let my finances dip below five cents. A nickel was my lucky piece, my coin to survival.

If I hit a town late in the day, all but broke and unable to search for work till the next day, I'd take that nickel and buy two copies of *The Saturday Evening Post* wholesale from a dealer. Then I'd go out and sell those magazines retail for five cents apiece and make a nickel profit. Then I'd go back and reinvest the dime for four more *Posts* before returning to the street and doubling my money again.

I would keep going back and forth, buying and selling, until I'd picked up $1 or $1.25. It would only take a couple of hours and was easy money. And you could live for days on that amount of cash.

So I used this gimmick many, many times.

Fishing was another lifesaver.

I always fished throughout my wanderings. That was one of the big reasons I was gaddin' about. I just yearned to see new fishing holes and catch different fish. If there was a body of water around, I'd find it.

Mostly it was just for fun. Sometimes it kept me out of hock.

39

Once when I was flat busted near Jacksonville, Florida, I got me a little casting rod, went out on the Indian River and caught a bunch of sea trout. I sold them in about five minutes. You could sell anything from salt water then, just as you can today. It was always good for a couple of dollars.

And so it went—a little time here, a little time there.

Over the years—especially as I got older—you might think I was an ambitionless so-and-so out for nothing but a good time. Maybe I was, but I don't see it that way. To me my travels were a priceless education. I was constantly seeing and learning.

Most of all, I found out how to take care of myself.

Besides, right or wrong, it was just something I had to do. I couldn't have stopped myself if I had wanted to.

15. Home Again, Off Again

AFTER A COUPLE OF MONTHS, TOWARD EARLY WINTER, FRED and I circled back to Paducah by way of Denver, Lincoln and Kansas City.

We'd had our fill.

We had seen plenty, done plenty. And we had fished—brother, had we ever fished! We missed very few bodies of water between the Mississippi in the East to the Colorado in the West, from the Little Missouri in the North to the Rio Grande in the South.

We caught largemouth and smallmouth bass in the upper Missouri, rainbow in upper Platte, more bass in Iowa's Storm Lake and browns in New Mexico's Chama River.

Our appetites were satisfied—for the moment.

I can remember the night I arrived home. The folks were happy to see me and put out a real spread.

I could see my mother was hoping I'd wandered for the last time, that I'd gotten the wanderlust out of my system. I could also see my father knew better.

"Good to be home, son?" he asked as my mother and sisters cleared away the supper dishes.

"Yes, sir," I said, "it sure is."

40

"For how long?" he asked.

We both grinned. I had more reason to smile than even my father suspected. I already had my next trip planned.

The only disappointment I'd had on the trip was when we crossed through wheat country in Nebraska and the Dakotas. The harvest was just in, and I discovered I had missed out on something—a pile of money.

Every year men from all over migrated to that country to help with the wheat harvest. Those farmers and ranchers would import all the men they could. There was plenty of work to be done and plenty of money to be made. The wages were $5 a day—a mighty big pay at that time. A man earned it though. The work was exhausting. Shocking from sunrise to sunset took a strong back. And living among that hired help—some real tough customers—took a strong head. But you were fed and paid well and could take a small fortune home.

So I made up my mind I wouldn't miss it the following year.

Meanwhile, I went back to my old jobs in Paducah with the pipe fitter, the gas company and the Opera House.

When midsummer came I was off for wheat country.

The work was tremendously tiring. But I was never so fatigued that I couldn't get in more than a little fishing. I was hitting every stream I came across every chance I got. I didn't pack any tackle, but that wasn't a problem. Cane poles only cost a dime.

After a couple of months, it was back to Paducah.

Then, in early spring, 1917, I went to Mattoon to spend a few weeks with my grandparents. It was a visit to remember.

16. The Big War

I'LL NEVER FORGET APRIL 6, 1917.

I was in Mattoon when I got the news that the United States had declared war on Germany. The moment I heard it I headed for the Army recruiting office downtown and signed up in the Signal Corps.

This was no snap decision. The smell of war had been in

41

the air for some time. I had decided long before that I'd enlist as soon as President Wilson and Congress said the word.

There was never any question which branch of service I'd join, either. I had picked it months—maybe even years—before. I wanted to be a flier, nothing but a flier.

Aeroplanes had always fascinated me. I can remember seeing a flying machine for the first time years before while standing in the backyard of our home in Madison, Indiana. I was awed. Now I would have a chance to find out what made those contraptions work and fly myself. I'd grow a mustache and wear goggles and let my scarf flutter in the breeze just like those slick boys on the recruiting posters.

There was no such thing as the Air Force back then. Or Air Corps, either. Military aircraft were under the command of the Signal Corps.

So I waited in line at the recruiting office and signed on for the duration for the grand sum of a dollar a day. I was twenty-one and didn't need any parental consent signatures or anything. I requested permission to delay induction for a few days while I visited the folks back in Paducah. Later in the week I reported to an Army reception center, Jefferson Barracks, just outside St. Louis.

I was shipped almost immediately to Kelley Field in San Antonio, Texas, for basic training.

Once there I made application for air cadet. This wasn't as easy as it might sound. At that time cadets were college boys. But I put in for it anyway. I had to have some references so I wrote home and asked some people in town to write these letters of recommendation for me.

Then I sat and waited.

I had nothing to do for three reasons. One was that I had to wait for action on my application. Another, was that Kelley Field was in a state of semi-confusion. And the third was that there were more men than they needed for routine post and camp details.

World War I was less than two weeks old and, as a major facility, I don't think the base was much older.

Everything was new—what there was of it. There was only one hangar and a bunch of X-type aircraft. Thousands of Mexicans were being employed to cut acres and acres of thick brush so air strips could be built.

They were putting up barracks as fast as they could hammer

42

nails, because thousands of soldiers were pouring into Kelley every day.

So I lived in a four-man tent and did nothing—no K.P., no guard duty. I made musters, ate, slept—and waited.

I became friendly with another cadet candidate named William McCurdy. He was from St. Louis and one heck of a good fellow. Besides flying, Mac and I had something else in common. We both loved fishing.

So we decided to put our free time to good use.

We went fishing.

17. *Colonels Fish Too*

MAC AND I HAD THE TIME OF OUR LIVES.

Little Medina River ran by the western end of the field and it was thick with fat bass.

We didn't have money to buy tackle. But that wasn't a problem. We got ourselves a couple of cane poles, some line and a couple of big treble hooks. For bait we used bits of yarn or pork chunks we'd saved from the mess hall.

So we bobbed for bass and, boy, did we ever catch them!

The fishing was going so good—and I mean we went every day—that I wrote home and asked my dad to send along my tackle.

One day I was coming back from the river alone around dusk, carrying five or six five-pounders on a string. A car came barreling down the road, and the driver slammed on his brakes as he passed.

Now this vehicle had a flag attached to a front fender, but I had no idea in the world what it meant. I was a greenhorn. I should have known that this was the car of the base commander and that the short, stocky man sitting in the back seat with an eagle on his collar was no one else but the old man.

He rolled down the side window.

"Where did you catch those fish, soldier?" he asked.

I was a real rube. I didn't even salute. I just walked over to the car and told him.

"You mean you got those beauties in that little river?" he asked.

"Yup," I said. "That's where I caught them. Want a couple?"

He sort of blinked.

"I sure do," he said, laughing a little. "What's your name and squadron, soldier?"

"Gaddis," I said. "Squadron 507."

He thanked me, and the chauffeur drove off.

The next morning we were having roll call outside the barracks. Our squadron had moved in from tents by this time. A motorcycle came roaring up in a cloud of dust. A messenger hopped out and handed my sergeant a note.

"Gaddis!" the sergeant roared.

"Here!" I answered.

"Get up here," he said. "I don't know what you've done, but you're wanted at headquarters—the colonel himself."

Mister, I could have passed out. I was scared half to death. I thought I was going to be shot at sunrise or something.

I jumped into the motorcycle sidecar and five minutes later was seated outside an office at headquarters. The sign on the door read: "Colonel Chase, Base Commander."

Finally the door opened.

"Come in," echoed a voice from inside.

Sure enough, it was the same man I'd given the fish to the night before. This time I knew enough to salute.

"At ease, soldier," he said. "Sit down. I had those fish for dinner last night and they were delicious."

He took it from there and we gabbed for quite a while, mostly about fishing. He asked all about me, then told me something about himself. He was from back East somewhere and was a West Point man.

"Would you do me a favor?" he asked. "Here's $25. Go into San Antonio and pick me up some gear like yours, will you? I'll have my driver take you in."

Well, sir, if I wasn't the cat's meow—being chauffeured in the base commander's automobile, flag and all. I was tempted to ask the driver to swing by my barracks area so the boys could see me.

We drove downtown to a sporting goods store and I bought the colonel a steel rod and reel just like mine, a casting line, three or four plugs and some bait. It all came to less than $25.

When we got back I gave Colonel Chase his gear and change.

"Thanks, soldier," he said. "That's perfect. I'll call you soon so you can show me where you take those big bass."

He did. And I did.

We went out a couple of times. The colonel really enjoyed it. He turned out to be a real fishing nut. We both caught plenty of bass and we couldn't get enough of it.

Well, what happened from then was that I got a permanent pass. I managed one for Mac too.

I was the talk of Squadron 507. After all, I was the colonel's fishing buddy, wasn't I?

18.   The War Hero

I HAVE BEEN ILL ONLY TWICE IN MY LIFE. BUT I SURE PICK the darndest times.

Things had gone smoothly at Kelley Field—too smoothly. A little more than a month after I'd made application for flight school, I was given an appointment for an interview.

I reported to a captain. I was real squared away by this time. I knew the position of attention as well as how to salute. Yes, sir, I was learning fast.

I came to attention in front of the captain and saluted smartly.

"At ease, soldier," he said, returning the salute. "Sit down."

He had his head stuck in my application. He must have examined it only a minute or two, but it seemed at least an hour.

"You don't have a college education," he finally said, frowning.

"No, sir," I said.

"Don't you know it's required to make application for air cadet?" he asked.

"Yes, sir," I said.

"Then why did you put in for it?" he demanded.

"I want to fly, sir," I said.

He just sat there and said nothing. I thought I'd had it. He

45

took at least five minutes before speaking again, and it seemed forever.

"By heaven, if you've got guts enough to put it in, I've got guts enough to sign it," he said finally, shaking his head and never once looking up.

Well, sir, I've got to say this was one of the biggest moments of my life. It had been a thousand-to-one shot, but I had gotten away with it.

Next came a strict physical examination which I passed with no trouble.

Mac had passed too and we awaited transfer to Austin, Texas, for an eight-week course at the University of Texas.

Then it happened.

The day before we were to leave, I was coming into the barracks after the noon meal when I fainted dead away in the doorway. It had happened just as suddenly as if someone had thrown a light switch.

When I awoke I was stretched out in an ambulance and felt awful. A medic was in back with me and gave me a big pill. It felt the size of a golf ball and I never thought I'd be able to swallow it. I finally did, though, and it must have contained something real strong because inside a short time I felt like a million dollars.

Well, sir, to shorten a long story, my appendix had burst and I had peritonitis. That's when the infection shoots through your system, and it was often fatal in those days.

As had been my history, I was lucky. I pulled through. And inside six weeks I was on my way to Austin.

The course was a stiff one—plenty of navigation and technology and mapping. But thanks to all the help the college boys gave me, I was doing pretty well—much better than I had expected to.

One thing about the Army then, and I suppose it's the same today: every time you turned around somebody was telling you to strip for a physical.

At the halfway mark of the course, I was going through one of these exams. Suddenly the doctor, probing around my belly, said, "What's this?" Well, without ever having felt a thing, the inside of the incision from my operation had let loose.

"Son, you're going to have to have this taken care of right away," the doctor said.

So I was shipped to Fort Sam Houston where I was cut and sewed again.

There was more recuperation; and delays and transfers. Finally I got orders to report to the University of Illinois at Champaign to take the same sort of course I'd been in at the University of Texas.

I was about two weeks short of graduation and winning my wings when the Armistice was signed on November 11, 1918.

You can see what happened, of course. The Kaiser had gotten word I was on my way over. So he quit and the Germans signed that peace treaty real quick. I had made one heck of a war contribution, hadn't I? Yes, sir, I was a real hero.

I guess I just wasn't meant to be an Army aviator.

But I had gotten a taste of flying at a test field at Dayton, Ohio, in between my schooling at the two state universities. And I knew that wasn't the end of it. I knew I'd fly someday.

I also picked up something else that's stayed with me ever since: a mustache.

I was discharged at Champaign—coincidentally, about forty miles from where I had enlisted at Mattoon. I visited my grandparents overnight, then headed for Paducah.

I was home—for awhile.

19. Riverboat Pilot

SEEING A LOT OF THE COUNTRY IN THE ARMY HAD ONLY MADE me hanker for more traveling.

So after spending a couple of months with the folks in Paducah, I was off again—this time as far as California.

Don't ask me why. I couldn't tell you then and I can't tell you now. I was just looking for something I haven't found to this day.

Even an old Model-T Ford I'd picked up couldn't keep me at home. Right after the Christmas holidays I headed south to New Orleans. Except for one detour, I pretty much stuck to the border clear out to San Diego before following the coast up to Los Angeles as far as San Francisco.

The trip was a unique one for me for a couple of reasons.

One is that it was the first time I took a casting rod and

reel along on my wanderings as well as my bamboo fly rod. The rod was a steel five-footer made in Connecticut that collapsed into three sections so I could pack it right in my bag. It was the latest thing out and suited a guy like me perfectly. The reel was Kentucky-made and fabulous, although expensive—setting me back about $25.

To me that collapsible rod and reel was a jewel, and I guarded it with my life.

I had a chance to use it right off. I made an exciting float trip down the White River, fishing for bass all along the way. It was a pip and I used it along with my bamboo rod every chance I got—which was plenty, believe me.

Another reason this trip sticks out in my mind is because I got to fish the Gunnison and Taylor Rivers in western Colorado—something I'd wanted to do for a long time. I made up my mind that I would and I did—sidetracking north as I swung west along the Mexican border.

I got in as far as Glenwood Springs on the Colorado River in the heart of the Rocky Mountains. It was wild, beautiful country and there were no cars or Jeeps to get in there. There were few roads anyway. You did it by stagecoach and horseback. But it was worth it. I enjoyed some of the most wonderful fishing of my life.

I had to get out of that country in a hurry, though. It was so unspoiled and strikingly beautiful that I knew if I stayed more than a week I'd have never left. It was nothing less than God's country.

So then it was on to the west coast and another reason I'll never forget the trip—my first crack at the Pacific. I got my first taste of going for albacore and yellowtail as I made plenty of trips with commercial fishermen all along the coast.

In a few months I was back in Paducah.

Something was beginning to nibble away at me. I was 23 years of age and had absolutely no idea of what I wanted to do in life. It was a vacant feeling at times—and sort of a frightening one too.

One day I bumped into Irvin Cobb. Within an hour we had rowed across the Ohio and were sitting along an Illinois slew with a couple of fishing poles in our hands.

Finally we got around to *the* subject.

"Now that the war is over, Vern, what do you intend doing with yourself?" he asked.

"Did it show?" I laughed.

48

"What are you talking about?" he said. "What's gnawing at you, son?"

"I mean you hit the nail right on the head, Mr. Cobb," I said. "I have no idea what I want to be, no idea at all. That's what's eating at me."

Well, we talked. And we talked some more.

We talked of my love for aircraft. But there didn't seem much hope there. There wasn't a tiny fraction of the opportunity in flying that there is today. There wasn't any commercial flying to speak of. The aircraft industry itself was tiny. Outside of military and barnstorm flying—also small-time—there was very little in that field.

And we discussed my confounded urge to roam.

Finally Mr. Cobb said, "Vern, have you forgotten something you told me years ago?"

"What's that?" I asked.

"That you were going to be a steamboat pilot someday," he said.

"I don't know," I hedged.

"And you never will unless you try," he said.

Well, sir, the very next day I set out to be just that. I signed on aboard a riverboat as a pilot's apprentice.

There was no pay, just room and board. And after four years of learning under a captain, a candidate would be eligible to try for a pilot's license. Instead of four years, I lasted just four trips on the Mississippi.

I started aboard a steamboat called *The Inland Queen*. She was essentially a passenger boat, but carried some cargo. After she burned to the water in a spectacular fire, I joined other packets and steamboats. The runs were usually from Louisville to New Orleans, with stops at such places as Cairo, Memphis and Vicksburg.

The Mississippi was quite a place. I saw a lot of things. The big cities were interesting and sometimes wild places. But what fascinated me more were the shanty-boat fishermen.

Anywhere from ten to twenty houseboats would be tied up together in a cove somewhere and the people aboard lived like gypsies. Money didn't bother them. Whatever they made was from fishing. If they had it, fine. If they didn't, that was okay too. Either way they had a good time.

They were friendly, carefree, gregarious people—my kind of people. I'd join them whenever I had a chance.

A stranger could walk in cold and those people would make

49

him feel at home right off. That he didn't know them didn't matter. He soon did. I mean they didn't care what your name was or where you were from. You were welcome as long as you were a good fellow out to do no harm.

And they could size you up in a minute.

If you brought along something to share with them, fine. If you couldn't afford to, that was okay too. They were tremendously generous people, quick to share whatever they had.

And did they ever know how to fish. They were masters at trap, net and trot-line fishing. I enjoyed them tremendously.

The steamboat people were something else again. I didn't go for most of the crews I worked with. The mates were generally rowdies and roustabouts. I was pretty much a square peg in a round hole. I've never taken a drink of liquor in my life. And I've never gambled outside of a little poker among close friends.

And there was plenty of cruelty aboard those boats. I saw more than one man get the lash of a hickory stick to make him move faster.

So steamboating was fun for a while, but I soon tired of it.

Maybe it was the people I was dealing with. Maybe it was the routine. I was traveling all right, but to the same places. The Mississippi goes only two ways: north and south. I longed to go east and west as well. Maybe it was the apparent endlessness of the apprenticeship. The end seemed a long way off and I was impatient.

I suppose it was probably a combination of all these things. I didn't want to spend the rest of my life doing the same thing with the same people in such a confined area.

The Mississippi is well over two thousand miles long and measures the entire girth of this big country. But it wasn't big enough for me.

20. Don't Fence Me In

I WAS LIKE A CHARACTER OUT OF A CHARLIE CHAPLIN FLICKER in the early- and mid-Twenties: constantly on the move in double-time.

50

I crossed and re-crossed this country. Then I crisscrossed it. And I probed plenty beyond our borders.

I went deeper into Mexico than ever before. I started following the Columbia River in Washington one day and followed it up into British Columbia. Before I knew it I was in Alaska. I worked on banana boats and sailed through the Caribbean: the Bahamas, the West Indies and South America. I even got clear over to Chile on the Pacific side.

And, brother, I fished.

I chased trout in Alaska's Valley of the Smoke, tarpon off Cuba, and bass in western Mexico.

And I learned.

Distance didn't have anything to do with it. I mean I learned as many lessons relatively close to home as I did a thousand miles away. Like the time I spent fishing with my good friend Theodore Hartquist in Peoria, Illinois, which was only 60 or 70 miles from home. I thought the world of that man. He was a wonderful person and up to that time the finest fly fisherman I had met. He taught me the finesse of fly fishing.

And so it went—new places, new faces, new things, new fish. I spent a day here, a week there, a month or two somewhere else.

Only once did I ever linger much longer than that.

I was in South Bend, Indiana, one day and read a newspaper want ad about a job that seemed right up my alley. There was an opening as manager of a gas plant in Mt. Pleasant, Iowa. Was this what I wanted to do in life? I doubted it, but it was worth a try. I had nothing to lose. I applied and got the job. It paid $175 a month and I stayed for nearly a year.

I found out from the start that it wasn't for me, though. Oh, it was pleasant and all. But I could tell my nomad's blood was still churning because I was traveling every spare moment —weekends, days off and the like.

My favorite retreat was cross-state in the Council Bluffs area on the Missouri River where I'd go duck hunting. That was a big thing along the many miles of bluffs in those days. That's corn country, of course, but many farmers made a lot more money from duck hunters than they did from corn. They'd give you room, board and guarantee your limit of thirty ducks for $10 a day. That was a lot of money, but duck hunting was a real sport and I truly enjoyed it.

A wealthy fellow named Chan Powers had gotten me interested in that kind of shooting a year or so before. My folks had moved to Decatur, Illinois, and I had met Powers there on one of my visits home. Chan was a national trap-shooting champion and had been on one of our Olympic teams. He wanted to learn how to cast with a fly rod, and I had taken him out on Lake Decatur. In return we'd hop into his Pierce-Arrow and he'd take me to many places along the Illinois River for ducks.

I had liked it so much that a little later I had gone into it in a paying way with a fellow named Foley. He had leased about twenty acres along the Missouri and we shot ducks for market. Those birds love corn, and we'd buy a whole wagon of it for $10 and scatter it all over. Ducks would come by the squadron.

So I was still on the duck hunting binge all the time I managed the gas plant at Mt. Pleasant and got in all I could at Council Bluffs.

That was the only trouble with the job. I couldn't stray too far. And, mister, I was getting plumb sick every time I flipped over another month on the calendar and thought of where the fish would be biting around the country at that time of year. I felt fenced in.

Finally I couldn't take it any longer. I had given it almost a year, hadn't I? And I still couldn't settle down, could I? Okay.

So I quit and began roving again.

21.   Give Me a Ticket to Anywhere

IN LATE FALL, 1926, I FOUND MYSELF IN KANSAS CITY.

A man has to eat, so I went to work for a radio store.

Radio was beginning to boom and this store was featuring a model called a superheterodyne set. It was a pip—the most powerful on the market—and sold for $57.50.

The commission was $15 on each one I could sell. And, brother, I sold them like hot cakes. I mean I really hustled. My idea was to work like the devil up until just before Christmas, then sit back and enjoy the holidays.

The store had two or three other salesmen who were radio and sound technicians. They'd collar a customer and spend an hour trying to impress him with their radio knowledge. Me, I didn't know anything about radio or sound so I would make my sales on just what the customer could see and hear for himself.

In less than two months I sold 90 sets.

A few days before Christmas I went to the cashier and asked for my money. I'd kept every receipt and my commissions added up to exactly $1,350.

"That's too much money," the cashier said.

"What do you mean?" I said. "I sold them, didn't I?"

"Yes," he said, "but that's too much money for any salesman. The other boys aren't clearing anywhere near that figure."

This old boy was sure an odd stick. And I was beginning to get teed off.

Mr. Smith, who owned the store, heard the bickering and came over.

"What's the trouble, boys?" he asked.

"Gaddis' slips add up to $1,350," the cashier said.

"Well, why don't you pay him?" Mr. Smith said.

"That's an awful lot of money," the cashier said. "We never paid out that much to a salesman before."

Mr. Smith shook his head and grinned.

"I guess no salesman ever brought us in that much business before," he said.

So I got my money—a fortune in those days.

Looking back, that was the first real money I ever earned—and probably the last outside of fishing.

So I celebrated.

I went to the big department store and got myself all dolled up—a couple of suits, a bunch of shirts, the whole bit. Then I dropped by the luggage department and bought myself a fancy leather trunk. I knew I'd be traveling again after New Year's, and this time I'd go in style.

First, though, I had the time of my life over the holidays.

I knew a lot of girls in town and dated a different one every night. We had a lot of fun. I'd take them to picture shows most of the time. Not only did I love movies, but all the good theaters then had big organs. And, boy, to this day I'm entranced by organ music.

Well, I'd had my fill of fun and relaxing a day or two

into the New Year and I got the urge to get moving one night about nine o'clock. I packed my trunk, checked out of the hotel and found a drayman with a horse and wagon.

"Take me to the depot," I said.

Beyond that I had absolutely no idea where I was going.

When I got to the terminal, I checked my pocket cash—not including what I'd packed away. Then I walked up to the ticket window.

"Where can I go for $47?" I asked.

The ticket seller laughed.

"You drunk?" he asked.

"Nope," I said. "Just tell me where I can go for $47. Give me a ticket for anywhere."

"Let's see," he said, scanning a timetable. "There are a number of places you can go for that amount."

"You pick one," I said. "Any one."

"There's a train leaving at midnight for Jacksonville, Florida," he said. "How does that sound to you?"

"It sounds fine," I said, "just fine."

22.　*I Strike It Rich*

WITHIN A WEEK I WAS IN THE BLACK BASS BUSINESS IN A little Florida town called Apopka. I was selling those bigmouth bass for 25 cents a pound and making myself a good living while having a lot of fun.

I had arrived in Jacksonville, all right. I took it easy for a day or two while I tried to figure what to do with myself. That's when I met some people from Wisconsin who were passing through and headed downstate. They offered me a ride and I took it. I had heard a lot about the fabulous lake fishing of central Florida and figured it was high time I tried it. So I ended up northwest of Orlando in Apopka.

A fellow named Johnson owned a fishing camp on Lake Apopka. I'll never forget him. He had retired from somewhere in Pennsylvania and was in his early sixties. He had lost an eye and had a vicious temper. But he was an excellent businessman and made a lot of money renting boats.

Johnson was constantly enlarging his camp and wanted to build a 100-foot dock. He offered me a deal. If I'd help him with the wharf, he'd let me camp on his property and build a trap where I could sell all the bass I was catching instead of just taking them for fun and tossing them back.

So I bought me a tent and put a floor in it. Then I built a 10-foot square trap along shore near the camp's entrance and got hold of a secondhand scale to weigh up my sales.

Days I'd help the man with his dock, nights I'd be out on the lake fishing. In between I was raking in sales. Those quarters added up in a hurry.

Meanwhile the big Florida land boom started to crumble. The whole area was going haywire. An awful lot of people had overbought property, and when the collapse came, many were left busted.

I became friendly with a lot of people in Orlando during the months I had been in that country. One was named Brown. And just about the time I was finishing up the dock, he stopped by the camp.

"Vern," he said, "how'd you like to buy that camp of mine over on Gordon Neck?"

Well, sir, I wouldn't have minded. Not at all. It was a steal at the price he was asking. There was a five-room house and a nice square covered dock sitting on about twenty acres of lovely lakefront property thick with orange trees. Brown was caught in the squeeze and asking only a fraction of its worth. But I still couldn't manage the price and told him so.

"That's all right," he said. "Why don't you go ahead and move in anyway? If you like it and can come up with the money in a couple of months you can buy it then. If you don't, you're not committed."

I couldn't beat that deal. And I didn't know the half of it. When I got over to Gordon Neck, I quickly saw how I could make some real money. There were thick mossy beds covering the water around the neck. It looked like heavy green wool. Beneath I discovered it was loaded with golden shiners. They ranged 1½ to six inches—tailor-made bait.

So the first thing I did was look for an assistant. I wanted a big fellow because I needed him strong enough to be able to throw a cast net.

I found exactly the man I was looking for working on a road gang. He was a Negro named Jess and he was the size of a small giant. We made a good deal and he moved right in with me.

We started checking out the cast nets. You know the type—7- to 10-footers leaded down with about 40 pounds of weights. A man opens the net, knots the long drawstring to a wrist and loops the weights over the same forearm. When he throws the net, it opens like a balloon and the weights sink it real fast, trapping everything in its path. When it hits bottom, the man pulls the net shut with the drawstrings and hauls in a mess of bait. In no time he can fill a truck.

It sounds easy, and it is—as long as you know how to do it. If you don't you can get in a peck of trouble. Those weights can take a man with them if he isn't careful. I could get a net out there, but my friend—well, he was just a master.

We used those nets first as a tool to clear 20-foot square holes in the moss. We worked like beavers and opened up about fifteen of them. It was hard work and took us close to ten days.

Meanwhile I had bought a hundred loaves of stale bread in Orlando, let it bake in the sun for a while and then stored it so it wouldn't go moldy. When we were ready for the bread, we'd soak three or four loaves in a bucket of water and stir it up like mush. Then we'd feed it into those holes in the mossy beds.

You've never seen anything like it. Those golden shiners came for that meal by the platoon. I mean you've never seen so many of those critters. And they were easy pickings. We'd just drop a net down and come up with hundreds of them.

We took bait like nobody's business—and what a business!

I had bait when nobody else did. The word spread like wild fire and we had customers parked bumper to bumper to get served. You can believe me or not, but I was taking in between $1,100 and $1,200 on a Sunday—90 per cent of it clear profit.

And that was only part of my business. I was selling more black bass than ever.

So between the live bait and black bass, I was in the chips. I won't say I was a millionaire, but I was beginning to feel like one. It wasn't long before I went and bought me a brand new car.

I wondered where this kind of money had been all my life.

23. *Broke Again*

"BLOW, YOU DEVIL, BLOW!" I HOLLERED.

It was the dead of night and I was lying flat on my belly beneath a fallen orange tree as all the fury wrought by ten thousand demons raged about me.

A hurricane was sweeping across central Florida and taking my budding fortune with it.

First the roof of the house went. Then the dock. Then everything.

In a few hours it was over. So was my dream—gone with the wind.

In the morning I found two boats of the small fleet I had built up, fished them out and lashed them atop the car.

Twenty-four hours before I had been just about set to finally buy this little chunk of Eden and settle down for a while. I don't know if I would have been able to stick it out. But I was going to try. Maybe, just maybe, I would have made it. I had sure given it a lot of thought the past month as I'd tried to decide whether to buy the place or not.

I didn't have to wrangle with myself any more. There was nothing left to debate. And I mean nothing at all, mister.

So I hopped into the buggy and pointed her west.

A day later I was catching sea trout in Tampa Bay. A month later I was clean across state, fishing for more sea trout on the east coast. I settled in a place called Sebastian Inlet, a little spot south of Cocoa Beach and what's now Cape Kennedy, about fifteen miles below Melbourne.

Between the land bust and the hurricane, Florida was in tough shape. And the scent of a national depression was in the air.

But I found I could make a decent living at Sebastian Inlet. I don't know about that spot now. I haven't been there in years. But back in the Twenties it was simply a paradise for fishing.

It's an uncharted inlet that averages about six feet of water at low tide as it leads from the Atlantic Ocean into the Indian River. A rock jetty juts out some two hundred feet into the

57

ocean and a sandbar lies about two miles off shore to provide an ideal haven for fish.

Inside were just about every sea creature you ever heard of, including some of the world's greatest sea trout. That whole body of water was thick with trout that averaged about eight pounds. All a man had to do was cast a surface plug.

The Shell Fish Company had just begun a good business deal which was starting to attract a lot of out-of-work people from all over. It had set up a big icebox and scales inside a 10x10 shack right on the beach. A fisherman would weigh up his catches and get a credit slip. Twice a week the people would pick up all the tickets and come back with a check. And with the sea trout market generally between 25 and 30 cents a pound, it added up.

I was averaging between $200 and $300 a week.

Living was no problem. I was one of the first to throw up a tent. And groceries were easy to get. You could make out an order every week and the company people would bring it back filled in a couple of days, merely deducting the bill from your check.

It was a good deal all around.

So I decided to stay for awhile and make myself at home.

24. *The Shark Fisherman of Sebastian Inlet*

THERE WERE SHARK IN SEBASTIAN INLET AS WELL AS SEA trout.

One afternoon I was casting off the jetty with a friend named Henry Hunt. The area was full of commercial fishermen—some with rod and reel, some with bamboo cane pole.

Suddenly a jalopy pulled up on shore and a man climbed out and walked down to the beach. He was carrying a basket, and when he got near the water's edge he pulled out a shark outfit and a chunk of beef.

He had about 150 feet of quarter-inch rope and began tieing one end around his waist. He baited the hook on the other end with the beef and threw it as far as he could into the inlet. Then he walked back and sat on the sand, 30 or 40 feet of the rope coiled in front of him.

"Look at what he's doing," I said. "He must be loco."

"We'd better go on over and set him straight," Henry said.

We set down our poles and strolled over.

"What are you going for?" I asked. "Shark?"

"Yep," the fellow said.

"If I were you, I'd take that rope from around my waist," Henry said.

"What do you mean?" the fellow said coolly.

"If a shark hits, he'll take you clean out to sea with him," I said.

Well, this fellow didn't take kindly to our advice. I guess he figured we were sticking our noses into his business.

"Don't worry," he said real unfriendly-like. "I can handle it."

We didn't argue. We knew he was determined.

We had walked about halfway back when Henry stopped.

"Let's wait here and see what happens," he said. "We can't leave that poor devil there. He'll get himself killed."

Sure enough, about twenty minutes later, this fellow stood up and began feeding out rope. In no time the line stretched out as tight as a bow.

Well, this old boy started to pull like he thought he could hold that shark. He planted his feet and leaned back at a 45-degree angle.

You can guess what happened. When that shark took off with the bait, no man was going to hold him. It's plain impossible. Talk about having a tiger by the tail! I'll hand it to this fellow for determination if not for brains. He hung on for dear life, still leaning way back, his feet furrowing the sand like a plow cutting through a corn field as he was dragged down the beach.

I've never seen a sight quite like it. Henry bounced to his feet and reached that boy just as he hit water's edge. Henry pulled out his knife and snipped the line, and the fellow fell back onto the sand on his backside.

Well, this guy was madder than a wet hen and began cussing out Henry to beat the band.

"I'd have handled him!" he bellowed. "I'd have handled him! Now you've made me lose him, confound you!"

We didn't say a word; just walked away in disgust. If that

boy didn't have sense enough to know Hunt had saved his life, it wouldn't have done any good to tell him. But, make no mistake, Henry *had* saved his life.

I know of at least two men who've been dragged off that little patch of coastline into the Atlantic Ocean by sharks the very same way—men who have never been heard from to this day.

Can you imagine—anchoring yourself to one of the biggest, most powerful fish ever created? You might as well put your neck in a noose.

I guess there are a lot of ways to commit suicide in this world.

25. *The Bootleggers of Sebastian Inlet*

THE BUSINESS END OF THE DOUBLE-BARRELED SHOTGUN WAS staring down my throat.

A mean-looking *hombre* was silhouetted in the moonlight, a finger curled around the trigger.

"Hold it right there," he ordered. "Don't move a muscle."

I froze. So did my friend George.

We had been walking along the beach waiting for the tide to change, leaving our tackle by a clump of palmettos.

This fellow had jumped out from behind a bush and scared us half to death.

"What are you boys doing?" he asked.

"Fishing," we said.

"Where's your gear?" he asked.

"Sitting right over there," we pointed.

"Come with me," he ordered.

We had no choice. This boy held all the cards.

He marched us over to some rocks and told us to make ourselves comfortable.

Sebastian Inlet, you see, was known for something else besides heavyweight sea trout and lightweight shark fishermen. It was also thick with bootleggers thriving on illegal liquor traffic during Prohibition.

What was happening here was that a boat was coming in

with a shipment from out of the country. It was waiting for a full tide so it could get across the shallow depths over to a narrow neck of land at the mouth of Indian River. Our escort was a lookout for the gang.

It was just as well we had made ourselves comfortable. That boy kept us company for close to three hours.

Finally the boat crossed the inlet and he handed us our rods.

"Okay," he said. "If you're going fishing, go ahead."

Then he slipped away and disappeared in the dark as suddenly as he had appeared.

Yes, sir, it was quite an operation. The holidays were coming up and I guess there were a lot of thirsty people in the country, Prohibition or no Prohibition.

The liquor—mostly Spanish cognac—was being shipped in night after night from Cuba and the Bahamas. Mobsters waited in high-powered cars and sped it on its way to cities like Louisville, St. Louis, Kansas City and Chicago. I often saw sacks—usually 18 bottles to a bag—piled four-feet high and lined up 100 yards long on that neck of land with three or four men sitting on top armed with shotguns.

The almost laughable part was that all this was clear out in the open and no one bothered about it. At least nobody did while I was living around Sebastian, although I heard later that there was a big scandal about it and the ring was wiped out.

But in late 1927 bootlegging flourished there.

And in an indirect, crazy sort of way I became sort of involved—at least a lot of people thought I was.

One day I met this fellow in town and we got talking fishing. Something struck me odd about him right off, but I couldn't put my finger on it. I suspected he was a bootlegger, but that wasn't what had me wondering. It was something else—like I had met him before or something.

Later that day a couple of friends grabbed me. They were shook.

"Vern, you're liable to get shot!" they jabbered.

"What do you mean?" I asked.

"That fellow you were with—he's one of the biggest rum-runners in the country!" they said.

They asked if I hadn't noticed something special about him, and I told them of the strange feeling I'd had.

"No wonder," they said. "He's the spittin' image of you, mustache and all!"

Well, sir, I got a kick out of that. I really did. They were absolutely right: that fellow could have been my double. I just kept my fingers crossed that mistaken identity wouldn't get me into trouble.

It didn't, but I sure got some strange looks around town.

I got to know this boy a little as the days went by. He loved to hear about my fishing experiences and I was fascinated by his bootlegging stories.

This fellow was clever. He had a rabbit-fast cabin cruiser which he'd run out to Cuba and the Bahamas. He'd pick up a barge, the type that sits so low in the water that you often can't see it above the waves. He'd load up the barge with liquor, hook it to his boat with a very long cable and begin towing it on the long run back to Florida.

The Federal people knew darn well he was bootlegging. The only question was how.

It would take him a long time to drag that load across the Atlantic, sometimes a week to ten days. And he'd be observed plenty. But they could never spot anything out of the ordinary. You have to be on top of one of those barges to see it, so the government men couldn't detect anything from a distance. If they approached for an on-board inspection, the bootlegger would release the cable and continue chugging along. By the time they reached him, that barge was a mile behind and he was clean. When they left and were out of sight, he'd circle back and pick up his drifting cargo.

"I'll never get caught," he would tell me. "If the Feds ever spot the barge and go for it, I'll cut the line and take off. That's the reason I have such a high-powered boat. I guarantee they'll never catch me."

I don't know whatever happened to him after Prohibition.

All I know is that he made a fortune.

Me? I was satisfied pulling in my $200 to $300 in sea trout every week.

I was content—at least for a while.

26. Hook, Line and Sinker

I FELT LIKE I'D BEEN SHOT. IN A WAY, I HAD.

I was walking along a pier in Tampa one spring morning and—sock-o!

Sitting along the edge not twenty feet away was as beautiful a fisherman as ever baited a hook. Now I had seen pretty women before. Plenty of them. But this one was stunning—a medium-sized brunette and a knockout.

She had a line in the water and was crabbing. I backed off and watched her for a while. She'd fix a piece of meat on the hook and lower it gently into the water. When a crab grabbed hold, she'd ease the line back up and drop that shelly crustacean into a small net. I had seen people crab thousands of times before. And I had done it myself plenty. But I studied that woman's approach like the whole thing was a revelation to me.

Man, she was something—really something. I had fallen hook, line and sinker, and I hadn't even met this gal yet.

I groped for openers.

"Isn't it awfully early in the morning for such a beautiful woman to be so crabby?" I said.

How was that for falling flat on my face with a gosh-awful pun?

That girl just stared at me coldly with a pair of lovely dark eyes.

Well, somehow we hit it off despite my awkward start. Her name was Ruby Haskins and she was in her mid-twenties. She was a well-educated woman and studied voice. In fact she was a talented singer and was soloist at her church.

We began seeing a lot of each other.

Ruby was a pleasant woman, the kind that makes a man feel important with her interest. She was also a marvelous cook. We found we had a lot in common—with one notable exception. It was ironic I had met her when she'd had a line in her hand because she had no use for fishing.

Still, I was captivated by her. And for the first time in all my thirty-two years, I began thinking of marriage. My brother and all my sisters had long since gone out and married. I had always figured I didn't have time for it. I was too busy roaming and fishing.

This girl had me thinking of it plenty now.

I had to make some serious decisions. What did I want to do with my life? Where was I going? I still didn't know. I was still floundering.

I had tired of my existence at Sebastian Inlet a month before and had returned to Tampa, a town I'd liked the little I had seen of it. I was just taking things easy and fishing every day. Sea trout were getting 30 cents a pound in the market, and it was no trouble catching 25 or 30 of those two-and-three pounders and picking up a quick $25.

Was this what I wanted out of life?

Or did I want to marry and try to settle down? Marriage would mean responsibilities. I'd have to get steady employment.

I was in a stew what to do.

I went out and got a job selling automobiles.

Meanwhile, I went about my courting and made plans.

Four months after we had met, Ruby and I were married in the fall of 1928.

For a honeymoon I took her fishing in Tampa Bay.

27.   Gillis & Gaddis

I HAVE A DILAPIDATED SCRAPBOOK CATCHING DUST IN STORAGE. Inside there is a long-since yellowed clipping from the Decatur *Review*.

It reads:

WILL OPEN NEW
HARDWARE STORE
Bryce Gillis and R. V.
Gaddis Form Partnership

Bryce L. Gillis and R. V. Gaddis have been completing arrangements to open a new sporting goods and hardware store in the space at 410 North Water Street, formerly occupied by the Pease Candy Kitchen.

Mr. Gaddis, who will be in charge of the sporting goods, is well known by Decatur hunters and fishermen because of his activity in those fields. He was in charge of the sports goods department of the Caldwell-McClallen store before it sold out recently.

Mr. Gillis will be in charge of hardware. He came to this city six months ago from Chicago, where he was in the hardware business eight years. He also had been employed at the Caldwell-McClallen store since coming here.

The story went on for a couple of more paragraphs telling about such things as how the business would be called "Gillis & Gaddis" and how a "gala" opening was planned.

To the left of the story, sitting under some type reading *"NEW STORE OWNERS,"* was a two-column picture of Bryce and me grinning like a couple of Cheshire cats.

We had nothing to grin about.

Already in hock up to our ears, we had to go out on the eve of our opening and scrape up another $20 to stock the cash register for our first customers. I guess our biggest product was moxie—and not the kind that came bottled.

It was spring, 1929, and it had taken a lot of spunk to get started in the first place—especially with the smell of bad times in the air.

Let me bring you up to date on how I had ended up in Decatur and met Gillis.

Times had gotten tough around Tampa. The auto job hadn't worked out. When people have to tighten their belts, the first thing that goes is the automobile—especially when a car was a genuine luxury item. Then I'd gone to work selling for a heating outfit—another brilliant choice of jobs. Peddling heat in Florida is like trying to sell freezers to Eskimos. So that hadn't panned out either.

About the only other way to pick up a few honest bucks around town was to fish, and I had made up my mind to go "straight."

Finally I got fed up.

"C'mon," I said to my wife one night. "Let's get packed and head for Decatur. Maybe I can get some work there."

My folks had settled there and had written that there was work around town.

65

So within a couple of months of our wedding, I was traveling again—this time with a bride.

When we got to Decatur I went to work with my brother Raymond for a packing company. I was a salesman calling on the grocery trade. Well, sir, that didn't last long either. I just didn't care for it much. I didn't know what I was going to do and tried to clear my mind by fishing morning and night in Lake Decatur.

For something temporary to keep us going until I could get my thoughts in order, I took a job with a local store going out of business. And that's where I met Gillis. We had both been hired by Caldwell-McClallen to help in its close-out sale. He was about my age and a regular fellow.

Near the end of the sale, I asked Bryce what he was going to do after the sellout.

"I don't know," he said.

"Listen," I said. "You know hardware. I know sporting goods. Let's open our own store."

So we did.

All we lacked was money. Between us we didn't have two nickels to rub together. We didn't let that stand in our way. Hard times be darned, we went out and stocked up on credit. First we went to Caldwell-McClallen and made a deal to buy on a pay-later basis what hardware and sporting goods it had left. Then Gillis headed for Indianapolis to see a hardware jobber and I made contacts with various tackle wholesalers. They said they'd help us. Then we borrowed some money to put a couple of months' advance rent on an empty candy store on North Water Street.

It was as simple and bold as that.

We opened that store without a dime—at least a dime of Gillis's or Gaddis's.

And it didn't work out too badly. We didn't get rich and we didn't go broke. We were carving out a fair living.

We went along like that for about five months.

It was fun for awhile, but I began to get a little bored. I was getting itchy feet again.

I felt confined. Both of us had to be at the store most of the time, one of us had to mind the place all the time. So, although I got away to fish and hunt from time to time, I didn't get away nearly as much as I wanted.

Most important of all, I knew this wasn't what I wanted to do the rest of my life. Like it had been since I'd begun roam-

66

ing, I didn't know exactly what I wanted to do with my life. All I knew was that this wasn't it.

So when the business got on its feet I popped the question to Gillis in late November.

"Bryce," I asked, "why don't you buy me out?"

"Okay," he said. "What do you want for your end?"

We didn't have much in cash assets. So we worked out an agreement where I took the company car, several shotguns, some tackle and a little cash.

And I went my way.

I had absolutely no idea in the world what I was going to do.

So I proceeded to walk into a fantastic business opportunity —an opportunity that would change the entire course of my life and for the first time give me some financial stability.

28. You'd Be a Natural

I'LL NEVER DENY THAT I'VE HAD MORE GOOD BREAKS IN LIFE than any dozen men put together.

And one of my biggest, most timely strokes of luck occurred no more than a week after I'd decided against trying to make my mark in the world of business as a hardware merchant.

A salesman from the biggest fishing tackle company in the country was passing through Decatur one day. He was a friendly fellow and naturally we got talking fishing.

"With your fishing interest and knowledge, you ought to be in my game," he said. "You'd be a natural."

I didn't give the remark a second thought. I mean it. It was said in a casual, offhand manner.

Inside a week, I got the shock of my life. A letter arrived in the mail one morning postmarked Kalamazoo, Michigan. It was from the company's sales manager and he invited me up to the home office for a couple of days.

I could have keeled over.

An invitation like this was quite a thing in those days. Money was already plenty short and jobs weren't easy to come by—let alone them coming to you. Especially good

jobs. And this outfit was king of the fishing tackle business—
the very best.

The frosting to the cake was that this job *did* seem tailor-
made for me. I could get paid for doing the two things I
enjoyed most in life: fishing and traveling.

Well, I want to tell you, I made tracks for Kalamazoo as
fast as the four balding tires on my car would take me.

I spent three days at the main plant, meeting people, seeing
things and being interviewed plenty. On the last afternoon the
sales manager called me into his office.

"Sit down, Vern," he said.

He was one of those slow-moving fellows.

We made small talk before he came to the point.

"Vern," he finally said, "why don't you go on home. We'll
let you know."

I exploded.

"Look, sir," I said, getting on my feet. "I've been here three
days. I've met everybody and nobody has given me a bad word
that I know of. You need a man and I'm ready to go to work.
So why in blazes should I go home? If you're interested, you're
interested now as well as two weeks from now."

I thought to myself: "Well, knucklehead, you've blown it for
good now."

The sales manager never said a word. He never even looked
up. After what seemed a leap year, he reached into the top
drawer of his desk and pulled out a contract already filled out.

Can you beat that?

If I had gone home to await his call, I'm convinced I never
would have gotten the job. He had been putting me through a
final test. He wanted to see how aggressive I was. He found
out. I grabbed the nearest pen and scratched my signature on
the contract before he could change his mind.

The salary was $75 a week and my territory was the state
of Florida.

It was too good to be true.

I had to pay my own expenses and there was no commission
to start. But $75 was excellent money.

"Take a few days at home and get packed," the sales manager told me. "Then you can work your way south to Florida."

He gave me a healthy supply of order books and samples
and I was off on the first real job of my life.

Only I never did get to Florida—at least not on company
business.

I returned to Decatur and packed my wife off by train for Tampa, where I planned to meet her in about ten days for the Christmas holidays. I packed the flivver and headed east, planning to cut across Indiana, Kentucky and the Virginias before turning south into the Carolinas, Georgia and finally Florida.

My first stop was Michigan City, Indiana, and I didn't make a solitary sale. In fact I never moved out of my hotel for three days. It was 22 degrees below zero and I was afraid to stick my nose out the front door.

It didn't take me long to start selling though. My company had a real hot item at the time called a "Stay-Alive" minnow bucket. It was for keeping live bait and was made out of some kind of unique material, something like a papier-mâché. They went for about $4.50 apiece and sold like hot cakes.

When I hit Lexington, Kentucky, there was a message for me to call the home plant. When I called in, the president heard I was on the line and grabbed the phone.

"Vern, there's been a change of plans," he said. "We've decided to send Bob Grant to Florida. We would like you to take over New York State and New England instead. Report to Albany. There'll be a new contract waiting for you. Good luck."

He should have sent the good luck to my wife. She was already in Florida waiting on me.

Well, I had no complaints. I was happy to be working, whether it was in New York State or the Aleutian Islands.

I had even less reason to complain when I got to Albany. The new contract included a handsome $25 raise—making an even $100 a week.

I was in New York and I felt like John D. Rockefeller.

29. Cecil B. DeGaddis

A BRIGHT IDEA STRUCK ME ONE DAY IN THE MID-THIRTIES. I decided to go into the movie business.

The tackle trade was going along just fine despite the Depression. My company had come along with some amazing inventions and improvements to keep sales humming despite the shortage of money. Besides, with no jobs around people had more time than ever to fish. In fact it was often a necessity. If they couldn't earn their daily bread, they could catch it. Every day was Friday in plenty of homes during that era.

Yes, I was a lucky man. Not only was I working, but the job had turned out to be exactly what I had hoped it would be: too good to be true. I was traveling and fishing plenty and getting paid for it—and paid well.

So I kept busy moving around my seven-state territory.

And that's where I got the idea of movies.

I'd visit dozens of local fish and game clubs in my area over the course of a year. I'd be in a town selling to one of the stores and the manager would say, "The local sportsmen are meeting tonight, Vern. Why don't you drop over and give them a demonstration?"

So I would. It was good public relations and it stimulated sales. The fishermen would see my latest line of tackle first-hand, get a gander of the job it could do, and drop by the store the next day to buy it for themselves.

Besides, I enjoyed these clubs. I really did. Show me a fisherman and nine times out of ten you'll show me a pretty good fellow. We're all a little nutty maybe, but we're harmless. Anglers are the neighborly kind of people I like to be with. We have a common interest and they're my kind of folk.

So I would have dropped by these clubs anyway, business angle or no business angle. It's like anything else. When he's on the road, a man tends to go where he thinks he'll be welcome and where the people speak his language.

A Harvard graduate from Atlanta will stop by the Harvard Club when he's in New York. A San Francisco reporter will visit the Press Club when he's in Washington. A duffer from Chicago will visit golf pals at a local course when he's in Miami.

It's the age-old story of birds of a feather flocking together.

So I'd call on these clubs and something would strike me every time. Fishing movies would often be shown. Even though I enjoyed the programs, all of the movies seemed to be the same.

"Old boy," I would say to myself, "perhaps you could make some better fishing movies, by using a little more imagination and filming more of the action."

70

Finally I decided to try it.

I told earlier how I'd been intrigued by photography since I was a kid in Owensboro where I had bought my first box camera. Now I decided to buy a movie camera and put together some films on my fishing experiences.

I was hooked on the idea. I couldn't lose. If nothing else, the movies would make a fine hobby. But I knew it would be more than that. I realized it would help my sales if I could show movies at these clubs that were better than any those people had seen before. I believed that the time was right for better ones.

So when I had a chance I began putting these films together. It was a lot of fun. I fished landlocked salmon in Maine, brook trout in New York and stripers in South Carolina. I also hunted ducks along the Illinois River, quail in the South backcountry. And all the while I kept the emphasis on closeup and unusual lens angles and action, action and more action.

I showed the films a few times and people seemed to like them. Word got around.

One day I was in New Britain, Connecticut, when a fishing buff from a local sportsmen's club stopped me on the street.

"I hear you've got some pretty good films," he said.

I said I had some movies and I hoped they were good.

"Sounds like they might be just what we're after for our next meeting," he said. "What's your fee?"

"What?" I blinked.

"How much do you charge?" he said.

Well, sir, that stopped me dead in my tracks. It had never occurred to me that I should get money for showing these pictures. I figured the enjoyment I got and the boost they gave my sales were payment enough. My mind started clicking. If people were willing to pay for the movies, I'd have more money to produce more and better films. It made sense.

"What can you afford?" I asked.

"How's ten bucks?" he said.

"I'll be there," I said.

And that's how I got started in the paid picture business. It happened as simply and casually as that.

I can't recall the date or even the exact year. But on a cold winter night in the mid-Thirties at the high school auditorium in that medium-sized Connecticut town, I went from amateur to professional movie-maker.

71

It really caught on. I started getting more and more bookings. And every cent I got I pumped back into the movies to make better new ones. The whole thing snowballed. The better my product, the more the demand. It was a sweet circle. It got so I made a real production out of it. I sandwiched this film between some demonstrations before and a question-and-answer session after.

Within a very few years I was getting forty times what I'd gotten for that first show. And remember, this was still at the tail end of the Depression when nobody had any money.

What pleased me most, though, was the way people responded to those shows. I'll never forget one night in a small New Hampshire town. I had just finished a show in a Grange Club and an elderly man approached me as I was packing my equipment.

"What's your name again, son?" he asked.

"Gaddis," I said. "R. Vernon Gaddis."

"You got it wrong," he said.

"How's that?" I asked.

"It should be Cecil B. DeGaddis," he chuckled.

Well, sir, that busted me up. We both roared.

That gentleman couldn't have given me a finer compliment than to mention my name in the same breath with that of the great Hollywood movie-maker, Cecil B. DeMille. But I guess that old-timer had a point at that. DeMille and I did have something in common. We both featured casts of thousands. Mine were fish.

30. More and More Gaddin' About

THERE WAS ANOTHER BIG PLUS IN MAKING THOSE MOVIES. IT soothed my conscience.

My tackle company was wonderful to work for. Those people were marvelous. They would let you do as you pleased as long as you produced. And that's exactly what I did—plenty of both. I produced and I did what I wanted. I'd work like a beaver for a few months, then take off somewhere for a month or two and fish. A man can't beat that combination.

Yes, sir, I was always popping down to Florida to get in some fishing. I had bought a 35-foot cruiser—a real yacht to me—that I ran all over Tampa Bay. Sometimes I'd even charter it out and take fishing parties onto the bay for tarpon, sea trout, snook and redfish.

Sometimes my holidaying would bother me a little though. I'd say to myself, "You're nothing but a lazy so-and-so, Gaddis. Sure you're making good money. But you could be making more if you were back on the beat instead of lolling around here in the sun."

My conscience was clear as far as the company went. None of their salesmen were bringing in more business than I was. Instead the gnawing was a personal thing.

One thing about me though—I'm resilient. That feeling never bothered me for long. I was having too much fun. Besides, I had learned long before that money isn't everything in this world. A man should have a little rest and relaxation along with his work.

Still, once in a while, this lack of total ambition had nibbled away at me.

Now I could forget it once and for all. Every trip I took was business no matter where I'd go. I was shooting film everywhere I went. I had to fulfill my duties as a big mogul, didn't I?

I guess I was doing what those psychology people call rationalizing. And, brother, did I take advantage of it. I mean I was really gaddin' about every chance I got. I didn't miss many bodies of water between the Atlantic and the Pacific all through the Thirties. I hit Canada, Mexico and Cuba too.

The farther I went, the more and more it made sense to me. The people wanted to see unusual pictures, didn't they? So I'd constantly be filming, filming and filming some more.

All the while I'd be seeing and learning. New people. New places. New fish.

And that's exactly the way I wanted it.

31. A Character Named Kelley

HALF THE FUN OF FISHING IS THE PEOPLE YOU MEET.

An angler crosses paths with all types—including the characters. They're the ones who flavor the sport with a few laughs. They don't mean to be humorous, they just are. From the moment they put a line into the water they attract trouble like a magnet. They're an all-thumbs, accident-prone breed unto themselves—thank goodness. I mean you or I could fish for a hundred years and not have the oddball calamities happen to us that happen to them in five minutes.

Take Raymond E. (Bud) Kelley of Buffalo, New York.

Here is a pip.

I must have bumped into a dozen characters in my travels through the Thirties. But Kelley easily topped the class. In fact if I had to pick an all-time all-timer of the Thirties, Forties, Fifties *and* Sixties, it would be old Bud. The jury wouldn't be out ten seconds.

Now don't get the notion that Bud Kelley is a buffoon. Far from it. He's a highly intelligent chap, a very successful businessman, and one of my oldest and best friends.

Just don't put a fishing pole in his hands.

That big happy-go-lucky Irishman was snakebit right from the first time he baited a hook. He was vacationing in the Adirondack Mountains in upper New York State in the early 1930s and stopped by a friend's summer place. His pal's name was Bill Kenmore and he was a fishing addict. Bud hadn't been there more than fifteen minutes when Bill had him talked into going for some trout in the Ausable River.

"Fine," said Bud. "What'll I use for gear?"

"I've got plenty: waders, jacket—the works," said Bill. "Help yourself."

Somehow Bud did. But it wasn't easy. Kenmore's dimensions were about 5-4, 120. Kelley stands over 6-0, 195. So try to imagine the fit.

Despite such a painful start, Bud fell for fishing—hard. In no time at all he loved the sport. He couldn't get enough of it. And he always had a thousand questions so he could learn more.

And that's how I met old Raymond E. We saw each other along the Ausable one time and got talking. I was impressed by his enthusiasm. We became good friends and have remained good friends to this day. He's one of the greatest guys who ever lived. He'd take the shirt clean off his back for you. He's a fellow who's always trying to help somebody—and getting into trouble every time.

Well, like I've said, Bud took to fishing right off. But that doesn't mean fishing had to take to Bud. Despite his devotion, he's no better fisherman now than he was thirty years ago. It's a shame, because he's trying so hard—probably too hard.

Over the years I've called him from a dozen places from coast to coast—often in the middle of the night.

The conversation is always the same.

"Hey, Bud! This is Gad."

Yawn.

"Where are you, Gad?"

"In such-and-such a place. And that's why I'm calling. The trout are really jumping out here. Nice 4- and 5-pounders. I knew you'd never forgive me if I didn't let you know."

"Stay right where you are, boy! I'll be there tomorrow and I want some of those beauties to be left."

"Okay. I'll be waiting on you."

Yawn.

"Hey, Gad?"

"Yeah?"

"How do I get there?"

I tell him.

"Okay. Now don't you budge. I'll be there by sundown."

And he is every time.

Just last year I called him from Lewiston, Montana. He was on the next plane and we fished the Bitterroot River for a week.

Take Bud to any body of water in the world, though, and I guarantee he'll be overboard within five minutes. Or he'll walk into a hole and drop clear out of sight. Either way it's a near-tragedy every time because this boy can't swim a stroke. And it's a shock every time to hear a splash, turn around and see only a hat floating in the water.

I've seen Bud fall out of boats at least twenty times, but

none was funnier than one day in Moore Haven, Florida, on Lake Okeechobee.

The water was very low and we had to pole our boat out nearly a half-mile before we could start the motor and get out into good bass country. Even there it was only three feet deep. We cut the motor and got our tackle set.

Bud popped up first and started to turn around. There he goes—*splash!* Mind you, we hadn't even cast a plug yet. Kelley splashed around before he managed to grab the side of the boat.

"Pull me in, Gad—pull me in!"

"Just stand up, Bud."

"I can't!"

"For heaven's sake, man! Just put your feet down!"

"They *are* down!"

What was happening, of course, was something not uncommon when somebody falls out of a boat and grabs onto the side—especially a non-swimmer. He thinks his feet are down straight, but they're not. They've curled under the boat in sort of an "L" shape. And it's tough to convince the man that his feet are not straight down.

So this foolishness went on for a couple of minutes.

Finally I said, "Bud, I'll bet you a week's pay I can reach over on the other side of this boat and touch your feet."

"Okay, wise guy," he said. "Go ahead."

I did and caught him by the toe. You should have seen his face. So he stood up sheepishly and that water was no higher than his belt buckle.

Boy, I thought he would die. And I thought I would too. That's when I almost fell out of the boat—from laughing so hard.

That wasn't the only time Bud had trouble climbing back into a boat on Okeechobee.

A bunch of boys from all over were coming down for a week of fishing. Three of us arrived the first day: myself, Kelley and another fellow. We were eager to go after bass. But first I had to get a problem straightened out.

I was going to be gone the next morning to drive over to Tampa to pick up a friend who was due in by train. The problem was what would happen to these boys while I was gone. Bud is helpless and the other fellow was even worse. He had absolutely no coordination at all. I had visions of them both drowning.

What really scared me was the powerful 22-horsepower engine we were using. The motors didn't have gear shifts then. You'd just start it and—boom, it's off! And making it all the more ticklish was the dike you have to pass through to get in and out of the channel. It's very shallow and there are rocks on both sides of this narrow passage. You have to cut your motor and paddle through. Otherwise you will shear a pin.

Well, I spent half the day explaining the motor and the whole setup to Bud.

"You're going to be running this thing tomorrow, so make sure you understand everything," I said.

He said he did.

"Okay," I said. "I'll take her out now and you can bring her in. That way we can double check everything."

When we got to the rocks, I shut off the motor and glanced at Bud.

"I know, I know," he said. "When we pass through the dike, shut off the engine."

"You're learning, old boy," I grinned.

I spoke too soon. I had warned Bud a dozen times never to stand in a boat when someone's starting this kind of motor. So the first thing he did when I started the motor after clearing the rocks was stand up. I shouted at him and he did get down before the boat took off.

Okay. We went about our fishing and had a pretty good day. On the way back, Bud took over the controls. When the flood gates came into sight I turned around to Bud, and he nodded at me knowingly.

"I know," he said. "Shut off the motor ahead. Don't worry. I'll cut it off in time. You know old Bud."

I did. That was the trouble.

The motor was wide open and the dike was coming up closer and closer. Finally he cut down on the throttle. But now we were within 40 feet of it, and the engine should have been turned completely off.

"Shut it off, Bud," I hollered, "all the way off!"

He turned his hand on the throttle. But instead of shutting it off he turned it wide open.

Zoom—*bang! bang! bang!*

Then nothing. We just drifted.

We had popped a propeller pin for sure. I tilted the outboard back into the boat and there was the sheared pin. I had

77

spares along, and when I dug for the pliers Bud leaned over the motor to feel the propeller. He gave it a little bump and that motor swung back over the side—and Kelley went right along with it, clear out of sight.

This was serious. The other time—when he'd gone over the side into three feet of water—had been funny. This was altogether different. We had passed the shallow passage and now were in 25-foot depths.

I looked over the side, and there was Bud floating to the top—and banging his head on the propeller as he surfaced. I grabbed him.

"All right?" I asked.

"Yeah," he said, gasping for air. "Just get me in."

"Okay, Bud," I said. "Take your time and catch your breath. Then swing your legs over the side of the boat and climb in."

He tried it, but couldn't. He had both forearms into the boat, but his legs seemed riveted in the water.

"I can't do it!" he insisted.

"You can!" I shouted, losing a little patience. "Just try harder!"

Well, we started arguing back and forth like a couple of tomcats.

Finally I gave Bud one mighty yank and—*rippp!*

That's when we discovered why he hadn't been able to swing a leg over the side. When Bud had gone overboard, a plug somehow had cuffed his pantlegs together and wouldn't let go.

That's my boy Kelley all over—a real honey who pulls one gem after another.

It finally dawned on me one day what a dope I'd been. I had never gotten a foot of film of Bud in—or *out*—of a boat. I knew how that man tore me up. It figured he'd do the same to my audiences.

The beauty of filming a character like Kelley is that a photographer is guaranteed to get the kind of priceless action and comedy he wants in no time at all.

The next time Bud and I got together was on the Kissimmee River near Lake Wales in Florida, and I made sure I had my camera handy.

A young guide was poling our boat, and he steered us into a nice little area thick with heavy grass and deep pot holes— exactly where bass can be found most anytime. I made a cast into some reeds and almost immediately the water began to swirl. A big bass struck, but I missed him. So I yanked my plug out right quick.

"There's a big one in there, Bud," I said as I reeled in. "Put a plug in that pot hole and try to get him."

Bud lit a cigarette and cast. I grabbed the camera beside me and started grinding away.

Right off he got a strike, and the bass hit hard.

"Now take it easy, Bud—real easy," I said.

He took it easy all right. He stood up, and overboard he goes—out of sight.

Splash!

Well, I'll say this for that boy. He was persistent. He never turned loose of that casting rod or the cigarette. When he scrambled to his feet he still had a firm hold of that rod, and the soggy cigarette was hanging lifelessly from his mouth. And on top of everything else, he was broiling mad.

Bud was really a sight—soaking wet from head to toe and his eye glasses dangling from one ear.

"I'm going to get that devil!" he swore, spitting out the cigarette.

The bass had gotten into some weeds and Kelley set out after him like he was going to trap him.

"Slow, Bud," I warned. "There's plenty of pot hol—"

Too late. *Whoosh,* right up to his neck.

Meanwhile, I ground away. I was getting every inch of this priceless action on film.

Finally Bud reached into the weeds and put a hammerlock on that poor bass. He was a big one—a 12-pounder easy—and Raymond E. plodded back through the water triumphantly with him.

When Bud reached the boat, he swung that fish in over his shoulder, like one wrestler throwing another. Then he climbed in himself, wet as a whale but happy. He stripped off his sweatshirt and grabbed that bass. Smiling like the cat who ate the canary, he held up the fish in victory so I wouldn't miss it with the camera. He didn't have to worry. I had filmed every bit from a wet start to an even wetter finish.

"That's what I like, Bud—finesse," I roared. "You sure trapped that baby!"

"Didn't I?" he chuckled. "Next time I'm going to bring my shotgun along."

That's what I love about my pal Kelley. He doesn't take himself so seriously that he can't laugh at himself.

And within weeks people were laughing all over the Northeast. That picture became the hit of my show. I put some light music to fit the film, and it fractured audiences from Bangor to Kalamazoo.

Like I've said, I was out to provide people with unusual movies. And, brother, I couldn't get any more original than this one.

There'll never be another like it.

32. *"Gadabout" Is Born*

I'LL NEVER FORGET YEAR 1938.

War was brewing in Europe. Douglas (Wrong Way) Corrigan headed his outdated monoplane from New York toward Los Angeles and somehow ended up in Dublin 28 hours later. Kate Smith introduced *God Bless America* to a nation. Spencer Tracy won an Oscar for *Boys Town*. And Joe Louis flattened Max Schmeling in one round at Yankee Stadium.

I remember it even better for two personal reasons—events that would play a mighty big role in my future:

(1) I got my own radio show, and (2) my nickname "Gadabout" was born.

Actually both phenomena were laced into one.

My appearances at sportsmen's clubs had been going well and a lot of people would say, "Vern, you ought to be in radio." That didn't mean a thing to me for a couple of reasons. One was that these weren't radio people. The other was that I didn't feel my show was suited for radio. It was all visual—demonstrations and pictures. A man doesn't watch radio, he listens to it.

That shows how much I knew.

One day I bumped into a radio man from WGY, the General Electric-owned Schenectady affiliate on NBC's Red Network of that era.

"I've been hearing a lot about your show," he said. "Fishing folks say it's pretty darn good."

"I'm a tackle salesman," I said. "The other is just a hobby."

"From what I hear it's a pretty good hobby," he said. "Ever thought of radio?"

I said no and gave my reasons.

"Let's go to the station and talk about it," he said.

Talking never hurt anybody, so I went along. And before I knew it, that boy had me lined up to do a 15-minute show once a week.

"Before I sign anything, I'd better call my home office and get permission," I said.

I telephoned the president in Kalamazoo.

"Sounds great," he said. "It should be wonderful exposure for the company. By the way, who's the sponsor?"

"We haven't gotten that far," I said. "I wanted to get your clearance first. But the boys here at the station don't think they'll have any trouble selling it."

"How much are they asking?" he said.

I told him.

"Heck," he said, "we'll buy it."

So my start in radio happened as simply as that.

The handle "Gadabout" came about just as casually.

When we were wondering what to call the show a few days later, one of the boys came up with the answer.

"Why don't you call him 'Gadabout' Gaddis?" he wrote. "That's a good name for him, because every time we're looking for him he's gaddin' about the country somewhere."

So that's how I got the monicker, and it stuck.

Funny, but I didn't like it at first. I mean all my life I had been called "Vern" for Vernon or "Gad" for Gaddis. The only other printable name anyone had ever called me was my given name—Roscoe. And thank goodness only my mother did that.

So, like it or not, I was stuck with Gadabout.

The design of my show was simple. I just gabbed about fishing—pinpointed where fish were hitting, offered a tip here and there, mentioned some of the latest tackle on the market, told a funny local anecdote if I had one, and answered mail.

Well, sir, the show caught on pretty good. I was no Milton Cross or Norman Brokenshire or Ted Husing. But I had a 26-week contract in my pocket and was off and running. And I wouldn't be slowed down until I got hit by some swamp fever.

33. Swamp Fever

I GOT SWAMP FEVER, ALL RIGHT—MENTAL, NOT PHYSICAL.

A fellow named Courtney Ryley Cooper wrote a story entitled "Anything Can Happen" in two installments in *The Saturday Evening Post*. It was about a trip he'd taken into the Everglades in Florida. It was a fabulous tale and I was fascinated by it.

The moment I finished reading it, I said to myself: "Gad boy, you're going in there too." And I did. Brother, it was as captivating as Cooper had written it was.

Before I tell what happened to me, though, let me tell you a little about the Everglades.

It's a wild, wild place—especially when I first saw it in 1939.

The Everglades is the only subtropical area in the continental United States, and it covers most of southern Florida. It starts below Lake Okeechobee and goes clear down to land's end on the Keys. It's about 100 miles long and 75 miles at its widest, narrowing to almost nothing as it runs down the peninsula in that upside-down triangle that's called Florida.

The federal government made most of the southern Everglades a national park in 1947—more than 1,300,000 acres below the Tamiami Trail. And of this country's thirty-one national parks, only Yellowstone and Mount McKinley are bigger.

The government people have civilized the Everglades some. You can't bring a firearm in there anymore. But they still won't let you go in too far unless you have a special permit.

Yes, sir, it's quite a place. An intriguing place. I mean it has everything—even a Seminole Indian reservation right in the middle.

The Everglades actually is a big limestone and coral plain covered with muck and peat deposits. It's all swampy, with lots of saw grass savannas and hammocks, island-like clumps of trees. Mangroves are what they are.

There's a lot of bird and animal life—some of the greatest

fresh water bass, tarpon, snook, redfish and sea trout in the world. There's also some shark in Shark River.

Many people are afraid of the Everglades because of all the stories written about the alligators and snakes and such. They aren't the real danger. Those critters won't bother a man normally if he knows what he's doing. It's the mangroves that will kill you. They all look alike and are confusing. You can get lost among them and never get out. That's happened to several people.

The problem is it's hard to keep a bearing on where you are. You can keep going around in circles. Worse still, you can go deeper into the swamp when you're trying to get out. There is a tide, but, since it sometimes flows in different directions, you can't follow it. To keep your bearings, you have to know something about the wind and be able to follow the sun.

But don't kid yourself, mister. What you really need is a guide. If you want to go any distance into those swamps you'd better have one. Otherwise you'd better have your will made out. It's true even today with the government controlling it somewhat. So you can imagine what it was almost 30 years ago.

That's why, when I decided to go in, the first thing I did was try to line up a guide.

I was in New York and had gathered a bunch of boys from Schenectady to go along. So I got hold of the name of an Everglades guide with a pretty fair reputation and wrote him. He wrote back that he'd take the group of us in for a week for $250. And here's where I made a mistake. When I wrote to agree on the price, I used company stationery. He saw I was with a big name corporation and promptly upped his price to $500.

We couldn't pay that kind of money—remember, this wasn't long after the Depression—but headed for Florida anyway. We figured to pick up a guide down there, although by now we were getting brave and foolish and beginning to wonder if we needed one anyway.

We were about a day ahead of schedule when we hit the Clewiston area and decided to stop at Bill Johnson's camp there to have a go at those bigmouth bass in Lake Okeechobee.

And there something incredible happened, one of those lucky things that have been my good fortune so often.

We told Johnson we were going into the Everglades and couldn't afford to pay $500 for a guide.

"Do you have any rags we can buy, Bill?" I asked. "I figure we might be able to get by ourselves if we can mark our trail by tieing rags on the mangroves."

"Sure," he said. "You can have them. But you boys need a guide in that country. And by coincidence I've got a fellow sleeping in the next room who just came out of the Everglades."

Well, sir, he was right. The man's name was Bill Morgan and he was somebody you read about in fiction. A fabulous character. He couldn't have been more than thirty-five at the time, a bachelor who had been trapping in the Everglades about 14 years. He used to bring out about 2,400 coonskins a year.

We figured this was too good to be true and barged right into this poor devil's room to wake him up. He was there all right—sleeping on the floor like a baby. I shook him and introduced the bunch of us. Then I popped the question.

"We're going into the Everglades for about ten days," I said. "Would you take us in?"

"I dunno," he said, rubbing the sleep out of his eyes. "Mister, I just came out of there."

We started sweet-talking him how much we needed him and how much we wanted to see the Everglades the way only he could show us.

Finally he weakened a little.

"Maybe," he said.

"What do you charge?" I asked.

He pondered that one awhile.

Finally he said, "Would a dollar a day be too much?"

This guy *was* too good to be true.

"Come on, friend," I said. "Let's go to our hotel so you can get a good night's sleep before heading out in the morning."

"Not me," he said. "I'm not going to any hotel. I'm comfortable right where I am. This floor is good enough for any man to sleep on. You boys go ahead. I'll meet you there in the morning."

"What about your gear, your clothes?" I asked.

"You see it all, mister," he said. He was wearing a pair of dungarees and a shirt and was barefoot.

We weren't about to let this fellow get away and we finally

84

convinced him, after a lot of talking, to come to the Clewiston Inn for the night. We put him in a room and locked his door. Like I said, we didn't want him to get away.

In the morning we stopped by his room so we could all go to breakfast together. And you can guess where we found him sleeping—in the middle of the floor.

We finally got going after stopping by Johnson's to get all our gear together and some extra supplies. Then we took off across the Tamiami Trail and out to Key West. There we hired a cook and rented a 60-foot work boat—complete with skipper —and four 15-footers outfitted with five-horsepower motors. All this for the sum of $350. The work boat would be our base of operation, where we'd eat and sleep. We'd fish mostly off the smaller boats.

Finally we were ready and headed the forty or fifty miles across the gulf to Shark Point. That's at the foot of Shark River which leads up into the Everglades.

Our adventure was off and humming.

We started up the Shark River and, let me tell you, this Bill was the greatest guide we could have bumped into in a million years. He knew every blade of grass in that big old swamp.

He took us about ten miles into the back country—way up to the head of a good-sized body of water which he called "White Water Bay." That's about as far back as anyone had gone in those days. And very few had gone that far.

It was a fascinating trip up. We saw all sorts of wild life from time to time—especially plenty of birds.

After a few miles the water changed from salt to brackish as it drained out of the prairie country and into the thick of the swamp.

While we were cruising around in the back country, we hit a little lake.

"This is Mud Lake," Bill said, "and I bet I'm the only man in the world who knows its name."

"How come?" I asked.

"I named it," he said.

Meanwhile, all along the way, Bill was sitting up on the bow watching that coral bottom carefully. He really knew his business. He knew coral could tear the props on a motor to pieces. The water was generally only about five feet deep, often less, but there were frequent water holes several feet deeper. You could stick your oar down into the water, prod, and the bottom was as hard as concrete.

When we got to the head of Big Bay we dropped anchor and moored between two islands.

Nighttime in the Everglades is an experience. It's something like a Hollywood jungle picture, except that what you see is real. The minute the sun goes down the area comes alive with noises—all kinds of sounds: birds screaming, wildcats crying, bull gators bellowing and tarpon splashing. It's fascinating.

So we couldn't sleep much that first night. But Bill did. When we began bedding down on the boat, I handed him a cot and blanket.

"Heck, no," he said. "I'm sleeping on this here table."

And he did.

The next day we started fishing and it was wonderful. That bay was a fabulous place and we caught plenty of snook and tarpon and a few redfish.

Late that afternoon Bill took us farther back into an inlet where he often stayed. He had a six-foot square platform built up off the water in the mangroves. How he survived the mosquitoes I'll never know. Bill had made it out of materials from the land, and that's where he slept.

We worried about that man, although we knew he could take care of himself better than we could ourselves. Still, this man didn't eat enough food to fill the palm of your hand. One of the fellows in our party was a doctor and he told us not to worry about it. He said Bill had been living that way for so long that he didn't require much food any more. And the funny part of it was that Bill was probably in better shape than any of us. He was slender but muscular and appeared in excellent health.

It's a wonder he had a tooth left in his head though. I mean this fellow gnashed his teeth in his sleep to beat the band. He nearly drove us mad at night. It was the final touch to that chorus of jungle sounds.

I'll tell you something else about him. He's the only person I ever heard of who could find his way around those swamps in the dead of night. It's tough enough in the day, but Bill could take off in the pitch black with an outboard motor with no trouble.

One night early on the trip he and Muff Morgan, a real estate man in our party, were talking about coon hunting.

"Want to go out tonight and see some?" Bill asked.

"Sure," said Muff.

". . . take a boy fishing! You'd be surprised how much fun it can be. Even a 71-year-old angler like me, and an 8-year-older, like Ray Kelly of Los Angeles, had a swell time talking about the how and why's of dry flies."

". . . even Uncle Sam didn't really stop my fishing activities. I always found a brook or water hole to test a line in. Here I am, in 1917, at Kelley Field, Texas, posing as one of the Army Air Force's most land-locked privates."

". . . that's me, behind the mustache. And those fish hangin'
off the pole are mine, too. This was a great day for fishing in
1927, on Lake Apoka in Orlando, Florida."

"Here's proof of one of my fish stories, and bigger'n me, too! This terrific tarpon came out of Florida's Tampa Bay in 1935."

". . . two whoppers (the fish, I mean) that I plucked out of Lake Okeechobee, Florida, in 1940. Looking at my pair of striped bass is Tony Accetta, former world's champion bait caster."

". . . some bigmouth bass I had fun pulling out of Florida's beautiful St. John's River, back in '49."

"How's that for a handsome group of stripers? I caught these at Massachusetts' Cape Cod in 1956."

". . . a nifty collection of Cape Cod's finest stripers, 1956 vintage. Helping me catch 'em were Dick Roderiguez and Beverly Wallace, known as New England's outstanding lady angler."

"I really caught the 'blues' this day! That's Vic Mion holding the other end of the string of bluefish we pulled out of Buzzards Bay, Massachusetts, in 1958."

". . . if there's one thing I enjoy as much as a good time fishing it's being surrounded by a gaggle of kids, and swapping fishin' tales with 'em."

Opposite:
". . . a pretty fair day's start while salt-water fishing off of a party boat out of Los Angeles, California."

"I'm hip to trout, and ain't this a nice string of 'em? Montana's *Big Hole River* is a good place for finding them, if you don't mind wading a while."

"That's me on the left and U.S. Commissioner of Reclamation Floyd E. Dominy on the right as we try our luck on the trout in Arizona's Lake Powell. This is one of our newest national recreation areas."

". . . floating the Green River in Utah, in search of some fine-finned friends. This 1965 trip was exciting and beautiful—and a lot rougher than the Blue River of my Indiana boyhood."

"After a long day on the water at Flaming Gorge, Utah, it feels good to warm up by the fire—especially with a nice catch of rainbow trout to show off to the guys. That cold and damp looking fellow on the right is our TV cameraman, Leslie Kovacs."

"My good friend Winston Mergott is just about to pull a largemouth bass out of Maine's Kennebec River. That's me behind the oars ready to offer moral support, or a net."

And they took off. We wondered if we'd ever see them again. I mean it. But, sure enough, back they came in a few hours, same side and all. If you or I tried it, we'd never have got back.

One morning on White Water Bay I figured it was about time I tried to take a shark. I had brought along a shark outfit—a shark hook, chain and swivel, and 100 feet of half-inch manila rope. I tied one end of the rope to the 4x4 stanchion on the stern of the work boat and baited the big hook on the other end with a jackfish. I hopped into one of the small boats and took the baited end out about 50 feet and dropped it into a spot about seven feet deep.

For two days nothing happened.

On the third day the cook had made up coffee and sandwiches and we were having lunch on the work boat. All of a sudden, like an earthquake, that boat darn near capsized. A tremendous lurch dashed hot coffee over all of us and knocked half of the boys sprawling.

Right off I knew what had happened and made a bee-line aft. Sure enough, that rope was stretched out taut from the stanchion into the water.

"I got one!" I hollered. "I got me a shark!"

I spoke too soon.

In less than a half-minute, there was a jolt and the line went limp. I gathered it in and it was exactly as I'd feared. That rope was cut off at the end as clean as if it had been sliced by an axe. Now that was brand new half-inch hemp. So you know it must have been a mighty good shark to have broken it off, hook and all.

And so it went, for the next week—a really fabulous trip I'll never forget.

I've been back there many times; once in 1950 when *Look* magazine was doing a feature on ten of us from my tackle company and I accidentally hooked a five-foot alligator that raised all sorts of ruckus. But that's another story which I'll get into in a later chapter.

The years have rolled by, but I never lost track of Bill Morgan. He's long since moved out of the Everglades. He got married and has settled not too far east in Homestead, just south of Miami. I still see him from time to time, most recently about a year ago. He's the same old Bill—except that he sleeps in a bed now.

That first trip to the Everglades would have been enough to

satisfy a lot of people. To me it was just a teaser. It got me licking my chops for more of that kind of wild country.

So no sooner was I out of the Everglades than I was trying to get into one of the most primitive swamps in the United States—Okefenokee in Georgia. I had been itching to try that swamp for some time and figured this would be as good a time as any.

You don't hear about Okefenokee like you do about the Everglades. But in my book it is just as good, maybe better. And if the Everglades is captivating, Okefenokee will darn near put you in a spell.

And on top of everything else, some people think it's haunted. Many natives have a superstition about that swamp—especially back then. They called it "Quaking Land." They feared it and wouldn't go very deep into it.

It's a big place, about 45 by 30 miles, mostly in the southeast part of the state, due south of Waycross. Part of it extends into northern Florida, west of Jacksonville. It is literally *Way Down upon the Suwanee River*. That old stream flows along Okefenokee's west side.

It's in the history books how lumber people tried to timber Okefenokee—there are plenty of bald cypress trees—going back to the early 1800s. But it's impossible because of the expense involved. They've never been able to drain the swamp.

The reason some people call it "Quaking Land" is because the ground actually does vibrate. The swamp has sink holes in it, and if some land is located over them it will just quiver. Loose ground and vegetation have built up and built up to form floating islands, trees and all.

So you'd better believe it, mister—it's wild country.

People down there tell a story about how a company of Marines came down with an idea to cross Okefenokee. Now if anybody is going to do it, it's the United States Marines. So this gung-ho captain brought his boys down one day and marched them in. The second day they marched out—the same side. Man, you just can't cross that swamp. It's impossible. Aircraft have crashed in there and have never been found.

The main part of Okefenokee is now a federal wild life refuge. There's plenty of game in there—lots of deer and bear—and some of the most beautiful birds you'd ever want to see.

So I wanted to get into Okefenokee in the worst way. But

88

here is where I got frustrated. Nobody would take me in. Oh, you could get a guide around the outskirts, the fringe. But I wanted to go way back in. I wanted to see it the way I had seen the Everglades, as few other men ever had. But because Okefenokee is such a wild place, and because of that "Quaking Land" superstition, I couldn't get anyone to take me deep into it.

I've returned and fished there several times, but never the way I wanted to. Now, with government control, you have to have a permit and be out by sundown. So I guess I never will.

Last year I made a picture in Okefenokee. Two of the fish and game men went along with us for part of the way. One of them had been born right in that swamp, on Billy's Island, named for a Seminole Indian. However, our trip took us only as far as the local guides usually go. We got some good shots, including some closeups of a couple of incidents with alligators.

We hit one area that was crawling with about fifteen small ones.

"Go ahead, Gad, pick one up," the guide said.

"But keep your eyes and ears open. If that baby starts grunting, let him go. His mother is around here somewhere and she'll come running and raise all sorts of the dickens with us."

Well, I picked one up and Bob Kimball, who was the cameraman on this trip, got a nice closeup shot of him. All of a sudden, this gator started to grunt and fuss.

"Turn him loose, Gad, turn him loose!" the guide hollered. And I did. We got out of that place in a hurry.

Later on we came upon a granddaddy of an alligator that must have measured fifteen feet.

"Let's get a picture of that old boy," I said.

Bob maneuvered his boat into position, got his camera down low and started grinding away. That old gator must have been camera shy, because he turned tail and took off—throwing a load of mud all over Kimball, his picture box and most everything else in sight.

We all had a good laugh—except Bob. He was a bit frustrated.

And I guess that's the best word to describe how I feel about Okefenokee—frustrated.

I'm intrigued by it and want to see it from the inside out. But, like I've said, I guess I never will. I've flown the Cherokee over it several times—a dangerous stunt, because if the plane went down it'd be all over. But flying over is no good anyway; I want to see it from down below, not up above.

After all, I've fished some mighty strange ways—but never from 1,000 feet.

34. Something Called Television

ONE FALL NIGHT IN 1939 MY TELEPHONE RANG. AN EXEC-utive from WGY was on the line.

"You have a lot of fishing movies, don't you, Gad?" he asked.

I said I did.

"How would you like to be on television?" he asked.

"Television?" I asked. "Do you mean my movies on tele-vision?"

He explained that General Electric had done a lot of testing and now was set to open an experimental station in Schenectady. NBC was about to do the same thing in New York and Philco in Philadelphia.

"We'll spread some sets around town for a starter and program a couple of hours a day," he said.

"Sounds like you may have something," I said.

"Want to be part of it?" he asked.

"Sounds like it might be fun," I said.

And it was.

The station's call letters were W2XD—to be changed to WRGB-TV in later years when television became a bigger thing.

And I was part of it as it grew. I had a 15-minute show on Friday nights and the format wasn't unlike that of my series today. Occasionally I'd do some demonstrating on camera, but mostly I showed my movies and narrated them.

Those first viewers deserved a medal. Talk about your technical difficulties! If something wasn't going wrong in the studio, the set in the home would be kicking up.

I can recall more than once being in the middle of a casting demonstration when one of those powerful water-cooled lamps would explode. Man, we'd all but jump clean through the studio roof.

The home sets were pretty awful too, burning out one tube or another just about every time you turned around.

Even when things were operating smoothly on both ends, the picture would be jumping to beat the band. And while it was flopping, I don't know why the viewers weren't flipping.

But they were a loyal breed and bravely bore along with all the imperfections.

The television people were as helpful as possible. Since newspapers didn't list the programming, the station printed the schedule on the back of a penny postal card and mailed it to every set owner each week.

Meanwhile, the operation grew.

First there were just a handful of sets around town. By 1940 and 1941 there were more sets and my audience multiplied. I could almost measure it by the amount of mail I got and the number of people who'd stop me on the street.

There soon was another way to gauge listenership. A Schenectady sporting goods store bought the show. I can't recall the exact details, but I believe the sponsor's cost was something like $25 and my cut was about $10. I've been told that mine was the second show ever sponsored in television history. Lowell Thomas had the first, a news program that was simulcast over radio and TV on NBC, New York.

The power of television advertising was proven even then. I recall one Friday morning I dropped by my sponsor's store. The boys there were upset. Somehow the store had overstocked on boots and couldn't move them. The storeroom was packed to the ceiling.

"Give me a pair," I said. "I'll put them on the show tonight."

By closing time the next day they were sold out.

Yes, sir, it was fascinating to watch television grow. It was all a wonderful, wonderful experience—really something to look back on.

That's why I sit back and smile to myself when I hear somebody say on a television interview, "Yes, I was on early television—1949, 1950."

How about that, Lowell?

35. The GIs

ASK ANY AMERICAN WHO WAS ALIVE IN 1941 WHERE HE WAS
when he heard Pearl Harbor had been bombed, and I'll bet he
can tell you. It's one of those memories that stick with a man
the rest of his days if he lives to be a hundred.

I was home in Tampa on a month's vacation for the holidays and driving along Bayshore Boulevard that Sunday when
I got the news on my car radio.

Mister, the wheels began cranking in my head.

I was coming up on my forty-sixth birthday—a little too old
to try to be an aviation cadet again. But don't think it didn't
occur to me, brother. Being realistic, I knew age also was
against me as far as any branch of the armed forces was
concerned. And that bothered me—tremendously. However, I
was determined to try. Where did I fit into this jigsaw called
World War II? I wanted to do something toward the war
effort. Something. Anything. The question was, what?

The answer was staring me right in the face. What I could
do best had to do with fishing, and fishing had to do with the
millions of boys that would soon be inducted into the service.
If my demonstrations and films were of interest to clubs and
on radio and television, why not to our GIs too?

By the next morning I had my plan mapped. I'd try to
enroll in the Army Air Corps. If that failed, I'd try to put
together a touring show to entertain our troops. If that failed
—well, sir, I didn't even want to think about that.

The first thing I did was get back to my territory, complete
unfinished tackle business and cancel my television and radio
shows. The second was to make application for an Air Corps
commission and take a physical, at Albany, New York. And
the third was to go to my tackle company's headquarters in
Kalamazoo and talk over my idea of doing a show for the
GIs.

The Army and the tackle company told me the same thing:
go home and await word from them. So I returned to Florida
and waited.

92

Inside a month I got the green light to go ahead with the service shows. My company had already discontinued tackle operations; the Navy had taken over the plant to construct instruments of some sort. But I would be retained as a roving ambassador. I didn't rove very far. I never got out of Florida.

The Special Services set up a program in which I'd tour the Air Corps camps, centers, radar installations and hospitals all over the state. I'd put on a two-hour show at a different place every night and work the USO clubs on weekends. In between I'd arrange with Special Services to take out fishing parties—often 20 or 30 boats at a time.

Well, sir, I have to say that this period—1942-45—was one of the most rewarding of my life. Those service boys were just fabulous kids. They were wonderful to me and I shared their laughs and their heartbreaks.

I'll never forget one night when I was playing an embarkation depot near St. Petersburg. The audience was fifteen hundred to two thousand boys headed overseas in a day or two. I was showing a movie of some fishing I'd done on the Ausable River in the Adirondacks. All of a sudden I heard the cry of a boy breaking down with emotion. A commotion followed and the lights were turned on.

The chaplain was in a huddle toward the back of the hall and he was motioning for me to join him. I did and that's when these 20-20 eyes nearly popped clean out of my head. The young airman crying was the very same lad who was appearing in the films I was showing. I had made the pictures about six years before in a little town called Upper Jay, and this boy had been a real Huckleberry Finn who had followed me, dug my worms and helped me get live bait. So he'd been in quite a bit of the footage. Now he saw himself on screen and remembered a life he wondered if he'd ever see again. I felt like crying too.

Talk about your long arm of coincidence!

Most of my moments with the boys were happy ones though —like one night I couldn't stop an audience of about twenty-five hundred splitting their sides.

Before I tell about it let me explain a little something about these shows. The design was pretty much the same old one: a casting exhibition, movies and a question-and-answer period. The last was always the toughest. Anytime a man invites questions he's sticking his neck out a foot. And with the service boys it was even more so, because they composed a

93

fantastic cross section of these United States. Their questions could be about most any fish or any body of water from coast to coast.

Well, sir, on this particular night I asked for questions and a youngster popped up near the rear of the hall. I'll never forget him, not only for his question but because of his squeaky, high-pitched voice.

"I bet I know a stream you never fished," he said.

"I wouldn't doubt it a bit, son," I said. "But let's give it a try."

"The Skunk River," he said.

That was enough to crack up some of the boys right there.

"Sure," I said above the laughter. "The old Skunk River—right outside Mt. Pleasant, Iowa. Many a 20- to 50-pound catfish I've caught there by the dam at . . ."

"He knows!" the boy bellowed. "Doggone, he *knows!*"

Mister, that entire hall just buckled at the seams. I mean that whole crowd roared for what must have been five minutes. I roared too—with relief. I had been lucky. The boy had picked one place I had known. I'm familiar with a lot of streams and lakes in this country, but no man can know them all.

So I had the last laugh this time. Another time the laugh was on me.

After a year or so, I had decided to put an added feature into the show: snakes. A friend from Tampa named Al was a snake man and a good one, so I decided to bring him around with me. He'd put a couple of rattlesnakes and maybe a chicken snake into a sack which he used to carry and give a tremendous exhibition.

And those boys really ate it up.

One night as I introduced Al on stage and started to back up—I stepped right on the sack of snakes. Boy, I'll bet I jumped three feet into the air. And I'll also wager some of those GIs are still laughing to this day!

The snakes really fascinated the boys—some too much.

One night I played a small radar camp somewhere in the back timber country. I slept late the next morning, and on my way to the mess hall at noon a lieutenant stopped me.

"We have a man in the hospital because of you, Gad," he said.

"How's that?" I said.

"Well, on account of your snake man, really," he said. "One of my men thought he knew all about snakes after seeing the show, and the first thing this morning he tried to grab one —a moccasin.

"He pinned it with a forked stick, all right, but didn't catch him high enough on the back of the neck. So the snake sprung his head around and bit the man. Luckily, we got him to the hospital in time. He'll be okay."

And so it went on my tours—interesting situations, interesting people. And the most interesting person of all had to be a fellow named Tom White—General Thomas D. White, boss of the Third Air Force.

Now I'm not a man to be impressed by titles. The fact that Tom was a Commanding General is coincidental. I'd have loved this man if he was a buck private doing ninety days in the guard house. He was just a fabulous man.

If I had to name the most interesting man I've met in this world, Tom would have to be at the top of the list. He was a six-footer with erect military bearing who had it all: intelligence, leadership, heart and wit.

The general was the son of an Illinois bishop and came from a long line of preachers. In fact his great-grandfather, Rev. Charles Dresser, performed the marriage of Abraham Lincoln to Mary Todd. Tom was a West Point man and one of its youngest graduates. He entered the academy at seventeen and graduated a year later in the speed-up program of World War I.

He had served all over the world and learned eight languages. He was an excellent flier and a brilliant intelligence specialist who headed up Air Corps intelligence for two years before taking over the Third Air Force.

Tom was a regular guy and always addressed his juniors by their first names. But nobody tried to take advantage of it. As one of his subordinates once said, "If a fellow goes into his office without knowing the facts for a briefing, the old man can toss him out the window without breaking the glass."

Well, Tom loved fishing. We'd sit around talking about it in his office, sometimes, at the old armory in Tampa, days; and we'd do something about it nights going for sea trout in the bay. In fact Tom's wife Constance, a lovely girl from London, liked to fish too. We often made it a threesome.

Tom and I had a wonderful friendship over the years as he continued up the ladder. Later in the war he commanded the

Far East Air Force and was aboard the U.S.S. *Missouri* when the Japanese signed the surrender. In 1957 he became top dog of the entire Air Force and served four years as Chief of Staff.

The general's success didn't surprise me. I knew he was a man of wise judgment from the time he had talked me out of fouling up the Air Corps years before.

I didn't really expect that I would get a commission, but when some papers came through, I discussed it with General White. After missing out on the action in the last war, I was ready to go into it, now that we were having this one.

"Turn it down, Gad," the general advised.

I glared at him, and he looked me straight in the eye.

"Listen, Gad," he said. "They're not going to let you fly at your age. Instead you'll be stuck behind a desk somewhere. They can get many men to do that kind of work. But there's only one man who can do the type of job you're doing for troop morale—and that's you. Stick to where you'll do the most good."

Well, that was Tom White all over: outspoken—one of the qualities that made him a great man. The world was a poorer place when he passed away from leukemia at sixty-four in December, 1965. I know that the general had to be right and that I would never fly with the Air Corps. Although I have never lived with regrets, for some time I carried a feeling of disappointment. So I did what Tom advised and kept doing the shows with the service boys. Let me tell you, it was a busy life and one of the most pleasurable and worthwhile things that I have ever done.

Like one night I had a bunch of airmen fishing near the Gandy Bridge in Tampa. These boys had got to feeling a little high in more ways than one.

In those days I was not as conscious of safety as I am today, but the boys were in a big boat and there was little chance of a man overboard.

We were using hand lines and weren't having too much luck. I had taken one fair-sized tarpon and they had none. The boys were beginning to get a little itchy, and that's when I decided to have a little fun.

Now you have to remember two things here: that it was dark and that these fellows had been imbibing.

I stuck my hand over the side and got hold of the line of the boy next to me and drew it in gently. Then I hooked my tarpon onto it and placed it back in the water. When the tide took the fish out to the end of the line, the boy naturally felt a tug.

"I got one!" he hollered. "I got me one!"

He hauled in his "catch" and I thought he was going to bust with joy. And no sooner had he thrown that fish into the boat than he started needling his buddies.

So I went to work on another boy's line and did the same thing all over again. I got the same reaction.

And finally I did it a third time.

Now this is where I made my mistake. Those boys started arguing as to who had the biggest catch.

"I'll bet you a dollar my fish is the biggest!" one said.

"Oh, yeah?"

"Yeah!"

"Bull!"

Then they started looking for their prizes to compare. And, brother, when they could find only one fish in the boat all Vesuvius erupted. Each accused the others of having thrown his fish overboard. Never mind war in the South Pacific or the North Atlantic. We almost had it right in Tampa Bay that night!

And so it went for more than three years—a wonderful, wonderful experience full of happy and other memories of the thousands of men who passed through those posts in Florida. I hope that perhaps some of them are again being entertained by the TV "Flying Fisherman."

Would you believe that over that period I received thousands of letters from those GIs? Well, I hope you do, because that's exactly what happened. I am not what you'd call a sentimental man. But I kept those letters for some time and every once in a while I'd pull some of them out of storage and go over a couple. It brought back memories of a very, very special chapter in this old man's life.

36. The Post-war Boom

LIKE THE REST OF THE WORLD, I JUMPED UP, CLICKED MY heels and shouted *Hallelujah!* on September 2, 1945. The war was over, and I rejoiced along with people everywhere.

Now it was time to go back and pick up where I had left off. And in no time at all, action was booming on two fronts: tackle and television.

My tackle company called all its salesmen back to work within a few weeks. But it was sticky going for awhile. The whole country was crying for gear and we could satisfy only a tiny fraction of the demand.

The problem was natural enough. There was the matter of the Navy moving out of the plant. Also, materials were still mighty scarce. And there was all sorts of reorganizing to be done after nearly four years of idleness. So it was impossible to start producing on anywhere near 100 percent scale right off.

Once we got going though—luckily it didn't take too long— things were never better. In fact the whole fishing tackle business was bursting at the seams.

The country had been through a long, tough war. Now it wanted to sit back and relax. And it seemed most of the people wanted to do it with a fishing rod in their hands. They didn't want a cane pole anymore. There was plenty of money around and people weren't afraid to spend it. They wanted the very best in tackle. And that's exactly what our company carried.

Probably the best way I can describe this frantic demand is by comparing the volume of sales in my seven-state territory. When I took it over in 1929 it was producing $20,000 in total business. By 1948 I was selling between $800,000 and $1,000,000 a year even though I had given up half of New York State by then.

I mean to tell you, mister, the tackle industry was really skyrocketing.

So was television. It was out of its infancy and beginning to come into its own. Stations were popping up like weeds. And with all of them starving for decent programming, it was natural that they turned to fishing.

Before you could say "'Gadabout' Gaddis" I had five different live shows on five different stations in five different cities in three different states on five different nights.

WGRB-TV in Schenectady—my old station—was first. WHEN-TV in Syracuse, WKTV-TV in Utica, WPRO-TV in Providence and WWLP-TV in Springfield followed. And that doesn't include a special series I did for WCNY-TV in Watertown, New York, for 26 weeks in the late Forties. They were all 15-minute shows with mostly big-name sponsors.

It was astonishing the audiences those shows had.

At first I had no inkling. I was curious about it. So I got an idea how to test it.

A fellow by the name of Al Stewart of Indian Orchard, Massachusetts, had made up a set of six lures for his friends. He owned the sporting goods store which sponsored my Springfield show and he gave me a set. They were spinning lures, and spinning was starting to catch on about this time.

I tried them out and they were dynamite. The nuts and bolts in my head started clicking. I went to Al and we got together on a deal where we could mass-produce them for $1 a set.

What I had in mind, of course, was a giveaway item for television. You see this type of thing done all the time today —including on my show (yes, sir, Al Stewart is still making my lures). But back then it wasn't being done.

My next step was to approach the sponsor of my Schenectady show—a national oil company with a string of gas stations.

"Ever think of doing a giveaway?" I asked one of its top boys one day. "It might not be a bad deal. It could bring a lot of trade into your stations. And it would be good public relations.

"Besides," I added a little sheepishly, "it would give you an idea if anybody watches my show."

"What do you have in mind to give away?" he asked.

I pulled the box out of my pocket and explained the lures. He seemed interested.

"You can't lose," I said. "Look, you buy them for $1 and sell them for $1. You're not costing yourself a cent, but you're doing fishermen a heck of a service because these lures aren't

99

available on the market. And even if they were, the general public couldn't get them for this price.

"Meanwhile, you're getting great public relations, encouraging new business and testing the popularity of my show all at the same time—and for free."

"Sounds good," he said. "They're pretty good lures, huh?"

"Yes, I wouldn't have told you about them if they weren't," I said. "I'll never endorse anything that isn't—including your gasoline. Money doesn't mean that much to me. I've tried these lures and they're fabulous. And they're timely. Everyone's starting to spin fish."

"Okay, Gad," he said. "Let me get in touch with headquarters and sound them out. I'll be back to you on it."

In the meantime I suggested to Al that he go to work and make up some of the lures. They were fine ones and I knew we wouldn't have any trouble getting rid of them even if this deal fell through.

A week later I got a call.

"Go ahead on those lures," the gasoline fellow said, a pitch of excitement flavoring his voice. "The home office bought them big."

"Fine," I said. "How many?"

"Let's try 500 boxes," he said.

Brother, I darn near dropped the telephone.

"You've got to be kidding me," I said. "You mean 5,000, not 500, don't you? You must have 40 to 50 gas stations in this area alone."

"Yes, Gad," he hedged. "But I don't know."

"Listen," I said. "I'll order the 5,000. If you don't sell them, you won't have to pay for them."

I called Al again and told him to finish up 5,000 as quick as he could. Meanwhile the oil company made up big advertising streamers to put in their stations when the giveaway announcement was made.

Finally everything was set and I made the introduction on my Friday night show.

"So, friends, just drop by your nearby station, plunk down a buck and the lures are yours," I ad libbed, like I've always done on all my commercials. "There's nothing else to buy. Your dealer just wants to say hello and get acquainted."

The telephone awoke me Monday morning.

"Gad, we've got to have more lures!" the frantic voice on

the other end of the line hollered without even saying who it belonged to.

It was my oil company friend and he was having a fit.

"My office is filled with $1 bills and the telephone is jumping off the hook with calls from my dealers demanding refills," he said. "I'm going daffy. Have your friend ship me another 5,000."

"By when?" I needled.

"By yesterday, smart guy!" he exploded. "The first 5,000 went within 24 hours of your telecast and we've been dry ever since."

Well, mister, I had found out in a hurry what kind of listenership I had. I'd be a fibber if I told you I wasn't pleased —and a little scared.

What worried me more, though, was the pace I was keeping —a different town every night for a television show as well as staying on top of my seven-state territory for the tackle company. I have to admit it was tough and sometimes would get to me a little. As it was, I had long since cut out all radio work and most personal appearances.

But what probably bothered me more than anything was that I didn't have much time left for fishing. And that just didn't go with me.

Oh, I was doing some fishing. I still had to get out to make the films I showed on my programs. And I had gotten hold of a little hideaway where I'd retreat and fish every chance I got.

It was a houseboat which Bob Grant and I bought. Grant is the fellow who took over the Florida territory for the tackle company when I was detoured to New York and New England. Bob is a marvelous man—a nice guy everyone loves. He's quiet with a wonderful dry humor that makes him wonderful company.

Well, sir, we bought this 30'x20' houseboat which we harbored in Georgetown on Lake George in northeast Florida. It could sleep four and was outfitted with a complete kitchen. It had a big outboard motor, and we had the time of our lives gallivanting all over the lake in that boat—even through the swamps. Man, we had a ball.

It's still a joke between us that Bob would do the cooking and I'd do the housecleaning.

"Yeah," Bob tells our friends to this day, "Gad cleaned up the place just fine. He'd head the boat into the wind, then open the front and back doors and let the wind do it for him."

I'll never forget that old boat. It was a pip. As a matter of fact Bob, who's remained with the company working out of St. Petersburg, still has it. And there's plenty of fond memories aboard.

So I was getting in some fishing in those years following the war. But it wasn't nearly enough. I knew I had to rectify that pronto.

That's when I came up with an idea how to kill three birds with one stone.

37. Me and the Wright Brothers

A DREAM CAME TRUE IN 1952. I BOUGHT AN AIRPLANE.

It was a red and white Piper Tri-Pacer, and it was a dandy. It was three years old, but to me it was the most beautiful aircraft in the world.

I'd have to say without question that one of the top moments in my life came on that spring morning when I plunked down more than $6,000 in cash and picked up that four-seated Piper Tri-Pacer at Wiggins Airways in Norwood, Massachusetts.

It satisfied a gnawing ambition of darn near 50 years.

A lot of people needle me and say I was with the Wright brothers when they made that first flight in December, 1903. Well, sir, given another ten years and I might have been. But as it was, the day Orville and Wilbur made history at Kitty Hawk, North Carolina, I was still in Mattoon, Illinois, 42 days short of my eighth birthday.

It was not many years after I left Mattoon before I saw my first flying machine. I can remember a lot of people thought it was a crazy fad engaged in by radicals intent upon killing themselves. Not me. I was fascinated by those contraptions.

I was captivated when I saw an aircraft for the first time back in Madison. Right then and there I said to myself: "That's for me. I want to do that."

And, brother, I did at my first opportunity.

That's why I enlisted in aviation when the United States got involved in World War I in 1917. I wanted to be an aviator. I thought those glamor boys with the goggles and scarves were wonderful.

Well, I've already explained how the war ended. And I did not get my wings. But I had gotten my first taste of actual flying. Training flights had given me my first glimpse of looking at the world from the outside in. And I want to tell you something: those Wright boys really had come up with something.

I thought there was absolutely nothing in the world like flying. And I still feel that way to this very day.

It's exciting and it's comforting.

It's just you and the birds and God up there. You can look at the tangled mess below and become a little objective. You can see things in proper focus. And it's so peaceful you can stop and think about what life is all about.

I had a sample of it in the Army and wanted more.

I couldn't pursue it much in the next ten years, drifting around the country and all. But don't kid yourself. I still had flying on my mind. And even when I didn't have much money on my travels, I'd save up a few bucks when the craving got too strong and pay to go up with a pilot.

There weren't many refined air fields in those days, especially outside the East. Mostly they were just grass strips—usually carved from not-so-level pasture land—where a couple of guys with planes would have staked out a makeshift landing field.

I'd go either to one of these fields or to a county fair where barnstorming fliers would be performing. Either place, you could give the pilot $2 and he'd take you up for 20 minutes, $3 for 40 minutes.

Most of them were using the old Curtis VX biplane, bought in war surplus. It was the same trainer I had handled in the Army. When these pilots found out I knew something about one, they'd more often than not let me take the stick for awhile.

I loved it.

I wanted to keep up with flying. I knew I'd be doing a lot of it someday. I didn't know how. I just knew I would.

It wasn't until I got my first solid job in the late Twenties and began making some real money that I had a chance to sharpen up on my flying. I took a lot of lessons on the side without anyone knowing.

In 1952 I got my license.

Besides enjoying it so much, there was a practical side to my flying. It made sense business-wise. My sales territory was a well-populated market, so the faster and better I could service my area, the more tackle I could sell and the more money I could make.

I don't mean I did all my traveling by plane once I got that license. I still used my car most of the time. But from time to time, when it was to my advantage, I could get to some place in a hurry.

Flying also permitted me to do a lot of fishing and hunting I otherwise wouldn't have been able to get in. I could work my territory all week, take off somewhere for the weekend, and be back on the beat on Monday. And nobody would know I had ever been gone.

Only my closest friends knew about my flying. I didn't feel like broadcasting it. In fact it wasn't until years later that my company found out. The discovery came when I flew into our national sales meeting one year. A few of the boys saw me coming in from the field. The word spread like wildfire. There was a lot of talk about it at the convention. No one could get over how I'd been flying all that time without anyone knowing anything about it.

You have to remember, flying wasn't anywhere near as common then as it is today—especially private flying.

That night, at the big dinner reception, the general manager motioned to me and I went up to him at the head table.

"I understand you flew in here yourself," he said. "Is that right?"

"Yes, sir," I said.

"How long has this been going on?"

"Awhile."

"How come I never knew about it?"

"I don't tell you everything I do, you know," I grinned.

"I guess not," he said, shaking his head. "Tell me, what else can you do?"

Well, we both had a good chuckle over that.

So I kept up with my flying—with the company's okay this time.

I flew when I could through the Thirties and early Forties. And even through World War II, when you couldn't do much because of the restrictions, my addiction only grew worse.

I was working out of MacDill air base in Tampa mostly and

was always gabbing with General Tom White and the Third Air Force boys. So I listened and learned—and yearned.

After the war it became even more imperative that I do more flying. Not only did I want to, but I had to if I wanted to keep up with the schedule I was on. So I'd beg, borrow or steal a plane when I could.

As I've said, tackle had become scarce and people all over my territory were hollering for it. I figured to distribute what little I had all over the area as equally and quickly as possible. And the quickest way was flying. I spent a lot of money renting planes. Flying became doubly imperative when my television work began to boom. When I found I wasn't getting in enough fishing time, a plane became a downright necessity.

That's why I went out and bought my own plane in 1952 and, as I've said, nailed three birds with one load of buckshot.

I still have pictures of that first ship with "Gadabout Gaddis" painted neatly in big letters on the sides of the fuselage.

Every two or three years I bought another one, clocking about 400 hours a year. I was making long trips working, vacationing. I didn't make them just once in a while, I did it all the time. I just about quit driving an automobile.

Now I'm on my fifth plane—a 235 Piper Cherokee. I got it brand-new in September, 1964. N8841W is a real beauty—red and white with "Gadabout Gaddis The Flying Fisherman" printed on the sides. I do between 350 and 400 hours a year in it.

It's a fixed-gear, low-winged four-seater that carries 85 gallons of gas and cruises at 166 miles per hour. A man can't ask for anything better than that. For example, with a good 40-knot tailwind I've gone from Little Rock to Boston—more than 1,200 air miles—without refueling in about seven hours.

You can imagine what a help that plane is in hopping around for my show. That's why it's the theme of the series.

My cameraman and I pile all our equipment into that little bird and take off wherever we have to go. No trouble. You can't overload it. It carries its own weight. It's a wondreful little ship.

I love to fly and land that plane.

The flying part is relaxing. And the landings are exciting. It's a perfect combination.

Now don't let that opening chapter fool you. That was a

freak happening. Normally you couldn't ask for anything more safe than a plane.

Let me tell you a few things about flying.

People are always talking about bad air experiences. They think it's risky. That's a lot of bunk. Nothing could be safer as long as you use your head and keep your plane in tip-top shape. If you fly your ship when you should fly and if you keep your plane in the order it's supposed to be in, you will rarely have any trouble. It's easier than riding a bicycle and one heck of a lot safer than driving a car. Motor failure is one in a million.

I have never had a crackup or even a near miss. And I know hundreds of other guys who never have either. That experience I had near Providence was the only time I've ever had anything approaching a bad incident.

The lopsided percentage of accidents is due to pilot error. Somebody doesn't use his head or takes an awful risk and— boom, you've got a catastrophe.

I never fly in bad weather. I could. My ship is loaded with all the latest instrument equipment. But I don't fly blind or by checkpoint. I don't have to. There isn't anything I do that can't wait 24 hours, if need be.

Radio facilities for aviation today are fabulous. You can get a weather check anytime you need it. You can go anywhere in the free world you want, anytime you want. There is no reason to get into trouble as long as a person keeps his wits.

The reason so many people get so shook up about the supposed danger of flying is that even the smallest crackup makes headlines. A plane crash is spectacular. Meanwhile, hundreds of people are killed in thousands of automobile accidents that hardly make the news.

I'm not blaming newspaper editors. A plane crash is more sensational than one involving a car. Besides, news is when something out of the ordinary happens, not something commonplace, and automobiles are involved in far more accidents and take far more lives than planes. The end result, though, is that many people have a warped fear of flying.

Well, let me tell you something. I hate to drive a car. I fear it something awful because so much can go wrong, and you don't know from one minute to the next what's going to happen. All I can think of is going 60 miles per hour on some highway with some character coming toward me doing 80 with a 20-miles-per-hour brain.

106

Give me a plane any day.

I hope I can fly my own ship till the day I die.

There's only one way you can ever ground me without my hollering about it. And that happened last summer.

Let the *Associated Press* tell about it as that wire service reported it at the time:

BINGHAM, MAINE (AP)—TELEVISION PERSONALITY VERNON (GADABOUT) GADDIS—THE FLYING FISHERMAN—HAS BEEN GROUNDED BY MOTHER NATURE.

GADDIS SAID TODAY THAT A TREE SWALLOW IS NESTING ON FIVE EGGS IN THE TAIL ASSEMBLY OF HIS PLANE.

GADDIS SAID THAT UNLESS THERE'S AN EMERGENCY HE WON'T USE THE PLANE UNTIL THE SWALLOW HATCHES HER YOUNG AND GETS THEM AIRBORNE.

Now, mister, there's a good reason for you—and about the only one I'll ever accept.

38. Cape Cod

WHEN GOD CREATED BEAUTY, HE DIDN'T FORGET A PLACE called Cape Cod.

It's only a small peninsula jutting out of the southeastern Massachusetts coastline, 65 miles long and 20 miles at its widest. But it's lovely and charming—and chockfull of fish kissing its sandy shores. After admiring and fishing it for 25 years, I finally took the plunge in the early Fifties and bought a little place smack on Buzzards Bay.

The move was as much practical as anything else. I had decided to give up the other half of New York State by this time, so my sales territory now consisted strictly of New England. And the Cape sits almost squarely in the middle of that area.

It was an ideal base of operation. I could get to Boston inside two hours by car and to just about anywhere in New England in the same time by plane. Only a few miles up the road was Coonamesset Airport, which provided my plane with excellent service and a pair of velvet grass runways.

And as accessible as that place made me to my dealers, it made my dealers accessible to me. That was equally important by this time because, believe it or not, the dealers were coming to me as often as I was going to them. My television shows were going so well that the dealers couldn't keep up with the demand for my company's line. So they would come down to Buzzards Bay and make a day of it, getting in some fine bluefish and striped bass fishing while writing their orders.

It was an ideal situation all around.

And there was still another big asset. There are two things in life that drive me to distraction. One I've already told about: driving a car. The other is paper work. And between television and the tackle business, I was buried in both. Well, sir, I found a solution to both on the Cape. But that's a whole other story that I'll get to a little later.

What I'm getting at is that the Cape suited me perfectly in so many ways.

And, brother, did it ever give me a chance to fish!

The Cape has some wonderful, wonderful fishing. That's one of the reasons I moved there. And my timing couldn't have been better. Striped bass fishing was just coming into its own there. During the war there had been all sorts of fishing restrictions, especially in the Cape Cod Canal. So the fish had a chance to fatten and multiply. The result: ripe, fabulous striper fishing. I mean you could catch striped bass just about anytime in season. From May to October. And some of those beauties were up to 50 pounds.

I'll never forget something that happened when I first moved to the Cape that points up what I'm talking about. I was in Boston one day and dropped by the old Union Oyster House. The counterman was a fellow I'd gotten to know over the years, Dick Roderiguez.

"Glad you dropped by tonight, Gad," he said. "I won't be seeing you for a while."

"How come?" I asked.

"Goin' on vacation," he said.

"Where?" I asked.

"I haven't decided on the spot yet," he grinned. "But it'll be somewhere I can fish."

"Why don't you come down to my place?" I said. "The stripers are hitting and they're as fat as tuna."

"No kidding!" he enthused, his eyes flashing.

"Of course if you'd rather go for something else . . ." I shrugged.

"Give me your address or I'll poison your chowder," he laughed. "You've got a star boarder."

Dick arrived the next night and I swear that man didn't sleep a wink. He was up shaking me before daybreak.

"C'mon, Gad, let's go!" he fussed. "Everybody in town will have an hour's start on those honeys!"

Now this boy was treading on something very dear to my heart: sleep.

"For gosh sakes, man, we just got to bed," I moaned. "Go back to sleep!"

"C'mon, c'mon, Gad—let's get out there!" he pleaded. "There won't be a striper left between here and Provincetown!"

"There'll be plenty," I said as I rolled over and got back to sawing wood.

I got up a little after ten and old Roderiguez was furious.

"You might as well go back to bed," he fumed. "There's no more fishing out there now."

"Don't you fret, Richard," I said. "There'll be more stripers out there than our boat will carry. You'll have so many you'll be throwing them back."

I fixed myself some leisurely bacon and eggs—complete with a second cup of coffee.

Meanwhile, Dick was fit to be tied. He didn't say a word though—just boiled to about 414 degrees Fahrenheit.

"Okay," I said finally. "Let's go. What's been keeping you anyway?"

The noon sun was directly overhead as we chugged up the canal and out around a sandspit that hooked about two miles into the bay. As soon as we made the bend into open water, we could see birds working over four or five schools of fish. I thought Dick would fall out of the boat.

We circled around behind one of the outside schools and let the wind drift us into the middle gently. Then those stripers began hitting left and right—and I mean healthy eight- and nine-pounders. In no time we had just what I'd promised: more than we needed.

When we got back to town we sold them all. At 30 cents a pound, we got a whole jar of money—which we immediately reinvested in lobsters. For three solid days we ate lobster morning, noon and night. Dick could really prepare them and I could really put them away.

By mid-week, Dick had his fill of stripers, lobsters—and me, probably.

Well, sir, that's the kind of plentiful striped bass fishing there was on Cape Cod.

Oddly, though, those stripers got me involved in some controversy that very first summer—and in such a nice peaceful atmosphere too.

Just about everybody went after stripers with heavy tackle and great big plugs in those days. They had the idea that it was the only way to catch them. They thought just because stripers were salt water fish that they had to use the big gear.

Not me. I started fishing light tackle from the start—regular bait-casting rod, bait-casting reel and 15-pound test line. And I used surface lures—fresh water bass popping plugs or short salmon streamer flies on a No. 4 hook.

People thought I was loco and didn't mind saying so. I got into some pretty fair-to-middlin' arguments as I preached light tackle and they insisted that heavy tackle was the only way.

I had the ace in the hole in any debate though. I was catching a lot more fish than anyone else was.

Even that didn't convince some of the pig-headed ones.

"Yeah, I see your fish," they'd say. "But you didn't catch them with light gear. You used heavy tackle but won't admit it."

Well, sir, some Doubting Thomases just won't believe a man no matter what. And the part that really irritated me was that most of these characters wouldn't take my invitation to come along so I could demonstrate. I guess they were afraid of learning something new.

I remember one fellow who wasn't though.

I was out on the bay by myself one afternoon when I noticed a man following me in a boat. He kept a distance, but when I moved, he'd move. That went on for almost two hours. I didn't think too much of it and went about my business. He appeared to be fishing, so I figured it was probably coincidence. On my way in, though, I couldn't curb the temptation for a peek at this fellow and routed my boat by his.

He waved his arms, so I cut my motor and drifted up close.

"Excuse me, sir," he said. "Can I bother you for a minute?"

"What's on your mind, friend?" I asked.

"I've been watching you and you've caught some of the

110

nicest bluefish I've ever seen," he said. "Believe it or not, but I've fished this area for years and have never caught a blue. What do you use?"

I showed him the outfit.

"It's just a 5½-foot rod with a little heavier tip than usual, a regular casting reel, a 15-pound test nylon line and this popping plug I picked up right in Buzzards Bay," I said. "I don't use a leader. Watch, I'll show you."

I made a cast and let it hit the water.

"You want to pop it slowly like this and hit your slack line," I demonstrated.

I turned the reel and hit it two or three times. Then I picked up the slack and hit it again.

Presto—a big blue hit!

Well, sir, I've never seen a man so excited in his life. He was a mild-mannered fellow, but he was so stirred up I thought he was going to capsize his boat.

"Where can I get some of those things?" he bubbled.

I had him follow me and took him to the sporting goods store in town and got him outfitted.

"How about coming out with me tomorrow and we'll do some fishing together?" I said.

And we did.

It turned out—and this is a real coincidence—that this fellow worked for the same oil company that sponsored my show in Schenectady. But that wasn't why I wanted to help him out. I did it because he was my kind of guy—not a know-it-all. He knew very little about fishing and admitted it. There are a lot of people in this game who won't though.

Meanwhile, my tackle debates continued. Some of those no-compromise heavy-tackle believers called me a lot worse names than crazy.

One night I was due to be a guest on a Boston television show. I caught some nice eight-pound stripers that afternoon, so I wrapped them up good and brought them along. I displayed them right on the show.

"They're sweethearts, Gad," the host said. "Where'd you take them?"

"Right in front of my place on Buzzards Bay, not more than four hours ago," I said.

I went on to explain my light tackle theory. Well, sir, that show got a ton of letters the next few days all saying what a liar and a fraud I was. That's how strong the feeling was in those days that it was impossible to take stripers with light tackle.

In four or five years, though, light tackle gradually became more popular. And today that's all you see on the Cape—even in surf casting. In fact there are all sorts of salt-water fly rod fishing clubs on the coast all the way from Maine to New Jersey. It's really taken hold.

And "taken hold" also sums up the way I felt about old Cape Cod.

I've mentioned only stripers and blues. But there were all kinds of fish to be caught there: pollock, bonito, snapper blues, tautog, mackerel, scup, cod, squeteague, sea bass, haddock, and summer and winter flounder. And you had to go only a few miles out for giant and school tuna, white marlin and swordfish.

It was just a paradise of fishing—and largely still is.

I loved that area.

I was never so busy in my life than during those years I lived there. But I can't remember enjoying any others as much.

39. Women Can Fish

DON'T EVER LET ANYONE TELL YOU A WOMAN CAN'T BECOME as expert an angler as any man.

Don't kid yourself. Given half a chance, most of them can. I know it hurts the pride of us male animals to admit it. But truth is truth and we have to yield to it.

I can prove my point.

I mentioned in the last chapter how I had found a solution to my driving and paper work woes on the Cape. The solution was a she: a wonderful girl named Beverly Wallace.

She became my secretary and my chauffeur. She even helped out filming movies for my television shows. She was an enormously capable and efficient young lady, a tireless worker who was of invaluable assistance to me.

But what I got a kick out of as much as anything was Beverly's fishing ability.

Bev was an excellent athlete when I met her, although not a

fisherman. She was only a little bit of a thing—about 5-3, 110. But she rode show horses, drove a golf ball half a mile and swam like a porpoise. I swear if some coach had gotten hold of her when she was in her early teens—she was in her mid-twenties by this time—she could have been made into another Babe Didrikson Zaharias. I mean it. She was just a natural in any sport, marvelous at anything she attempted.

Bev proved it by the way she took to fishing. She hadn't done any before, but became interested in it working for me. So she took it up and in no time became a real pro. She must have won at least 50 trophies and plaques for fishing within the next few years. She'd beat men and women alike in those big salt water tournaments on the Cape. She'd win at surf casting and bait casting, at the biggest bass caught, at the most bass caught.

She became so accomplished that I worked her into two or three of my films to let people know how well a woman can fish.

Everything Beverly touched turned to magic.

Like the first time I met her. She was a lifeguard on a beach and came over to look at my boat. I was on my way out to fool around with some still-photography.

"Why don't you pose a little by the motor there and I'll make a few pictures?" I suggested.

She thought I was kidding and laughed. Finally she posed and I shot an entire role of color film.

Well, sir, those pictures came out so well that I sent them to the motor manufacturer and the company bought them to use in advertising.

Like I say, she was a natural.

Take radio and television. She knew nothing about their behind-the-scenes workings at first. I'll never forget the first time I put her on the air. There was an all-night radio show on WBZ in Boston at that time called *The Slim Pickens Show*. They had been after me to drop by to gab a little about fishing, so one night I did.

"Slim," I said right on the air, "I have an accomplished young angler along with me in the studio tonight who proves women can fish expertly. Meet Beverly Wallace."

"Hello, Beverly," Slim said.

Nothing. Absolutely nothing.

Bev just froze. There was panic in her eyes and she couldn't say a word. Not even a syllable. It was the greatest case of "mike fright" I ever saw in my life. Slim and I just roared. Then Beverly began to laugh. That untied her tongue and it ended up a wonderful show. I had intended to stay for only a few minutes. Instead we were there until 4 A.M.

Bev's air presence improved like nothing you ever saw. She got to be able to handle herself so well that I often used her on many of my television shows to interview guests. She was a master at dropping a cue to bail someone out—including me at times—and could have handled the show alone if I had let her.

And that was that girl's only trouble. She got so gosh darn good that I was expecting the sponsors to fire me and hire her any day.

That went for her fishing too. She was starting to out-fish me. And that just wouldn't do.

Seriously, though, Beverly was priceless and I couldn't have gotten through that grind of a schedule I had in the early and mid-Fifties without her. She took an awful lot of the burden off my shoulders.

But, like any female, she ended up spoiling it. She went out one day and got herself married. Today, she is Mrs. Dave Gouger of Buzzards Bay, Massachusetts.

Well, I guess no woman is perfect.

40. I Outsmart Myself

MAYBE I GOT TOO BIG FOR MY BRITCHES.

Things had been going well for me—too well. I should have known that's the time a man's got to look out.

Tackle sales were booming, so much so that the company began to cut down our territories. By the middle 1950s they had whittled my sales area to just Massachusetts, Rhode Island, and Connecticut, and that was enough.

I had also started picking up some real money working the outdoor and sportsmen shows in the big cities in the East and Midwest. I had worked this circuit before the war, setting up booths and putting on displays for my tackle company. And I was still doing some of this. But now I had also become a part of the so-called feature talent. I would be master of ceremonies or put on a casting exhibition for a show.

I had long since given up most of my private club appearances. But the big shows were something else again. Not only was the circuit's money hard to turn down, but I enjoyed it tremendously. The interest of the big crowds was stimulating.

Then there was television—was there *ever* television!

And that's where I outsmarted myself.

I was doing as many as five live television shows a week in five different towns. It was a rugged grind, but I loved it. Gnawing away at me, though, was the question of how I could do the work bigger and better—and easier. Now I'm not talking about cutting corners. I mean I was looking for a way to accomplish even more on television by channeling my energy instead of running around like a gander with his head chopped off.

The answer, of course, was simple: syndication.

Just about the time this was crystallizing in my mind, and I was scolding myself that I ought to be doing something about it, I was approached on the subject by a small television production company.

Coincidence? Heck, no. I thought it was destiny!

The plan these people had seemed like a good one, and I went for it. We put together twenty-six 15-minute shows in black and white. They weren't half bad either. And that's just it. To be good, I had to put a lot of time into them. I was doing quite a bit of editing on the old films and taking some new ones around the country. I fished for trout in the East, bass in the Southwest, blue gill in the Midwest and even did a rattlesnake hunt near Sarasota, Florida.

There are only 24 hours in a day, so something had to give. And what gave were my nightly live shows. That figured. As much as I loved television, I didn't want to give up my other interests. Besides, the very reason I was getting into syndication was to avoid the grind of a different show and town every night. So I gave up all the live shows except the one in Schenectady.

Well, this is where I made the prize boner of my life. I won't go into the reasons, but the TV show with the new production company was something less than a smash success. I wasn't happy with the operation and sold out at my first opportunity. I've never been able to shake the bones of that old skeleton out of my closet to this day. Incidentally, episodes

115

of that old series still pop up around the country from time to time.

Now don't get the idea that this had been a tragedy in the roller coaster life and times of R. V. Gaddis.

I had learned from it—things that would help me in later years. I knew it and chalked it up to experience. And it hadn't cost me all that much financially because I still had more than enough going for me, selling tackle and appearing in shows. I also still had the Schenectady television program—and, believe it or not, the lures were still selling.

But I have to admit one show a week didn't satisfy my TV appetite. I craved more.

A sensible question might be why didn't I simply go back and pick up my old shows.

There were at least three good reasons.

One was that it wouldn't have been as easy as it might sound. A man can quit a job a lot easier than he can get it back.

Another was that I didn't really want them again. The town-a-night schedule was a little too much.

And finally I had my heart set on a syndicated show and was more convinced than ever that it could be successful if handled properly. My original idea had been right; only the execution wrong.

Meanwhile, I fussed and I fretted.

Then came a steak dinner one night that changed everything.

41. A Non-fisherman Named Russo

"GAD, I'M TAKING FRANCES OUT FOR DINNER TONIGHT. WHY don't you join us?"

The invitation was made by a good friend and wonderful fellow named Paul Adanti. He was—and still is—vice-president and general manager of WHEN radio and television, the Syracuse station that had carried my TV show for many years. I had known Paul since 1938, when I had broken into

116

broadcasting on WGY, Schenectady, where he was a control engineer, and we had remained close friends over the years.

"Okay," I said. "Where?"

"The Hotel Syracuse," he said.

"Who's buying?" I asked.

"I am," he said.

"Mister, you must have something on your mind," I needled.

"Just a steak," he smiled. "Let's make it about 8 o'clock."

"Fine," I said.

Paul wasn't telling the whole truth.

He *did* have more on his mind than a steak. It would be dinner for four, not three. And the get-together wasn't at all as casual as Paul had made it sound. That old schemer had been plotting it for months.

The clock pointed to exactly 8 when I walked into the lobby and spotted the Adantis talking with a fellow I didn't know.

"Gadabout Gaddis, meet Nick Russo," Paul introduced as I joined them.

The four of us made small talk.

"Okay," Paul said finally. "Let's eat."

Nick and I looked at each other a bit awkwardly. As I discovered later, each of us had been under the impression that he was going to dine with the Adantis alone.

Let me give you some background.

Paul had believed in my dream of a syndicated fishing show just as much as I. He had always been one of my boosters to a fault. He was always bending people's ears about me— including a pair belonging to Nick Russo.

Russo was then New England representative for National Telefilm Associates and worked out of Boston.

"Nick, I know a guy who'd make a great TV show," Adanti had bugged him months before. "Put him in a can, ship him nationwide and you'll make yourself a million."

"Sure, sure," Nick had said, trying to brush aside the matter politely.

I know what must have gone through Russo's mind. People in every phase of show business are always being collared by well-meaning but self-appointed talent scouts. Each has somebody he's convinced will stand the world on its ear if given half a chance.

Nick must have thought: "Oh, brother. Here we go again."

Of course he knew that Paul was in television and therefore

was a better judge of talent than most. But he also knew that because of the Adanti-Gaddis friendship, Paul's judgment was probably more than a little prejudiced.

Besides, Nick knew little about fishing and couldn't have cared less. So Russo had all but forgotten Adanti's suggestion —and hoped Paul had too. Obviously persistent Paul hadn't. He had merely waited until the next time Nick came to town. Then he proposed "joining Frances and me for dinner."

The result: four people sitting around a table nibbling steaks a little uncomfortably.

The syndication matter came up, of course. Paul made sure of that. He approached it with typical Adanti delicacy.

"Russo, when are you going to get smart and syndicate Gad like I told you?" he said.

I almost crawled under the table.

Nick didn't even blink. He's a little guy and sharp as the devil. He sucked in an ulcer and fielded the question nicely.

"Okay," he said. "Let's talk a little about it."

I gave my ideas.

"When you're in Boston someday, why don't you drop by the office?" Nick said when I let him up for air. "I'd like to talk this over some more."

I did and we did.

The result was that Russo lined me up with a weekly show on Boston's WHDH-TV.

The format was the same as usual: gabbing and movies. But it was unwieldy in that my time was indefinite. It was jammed between the Wednesday night fights and the 11 P.M. news. I might have five minutes, I might have twenty. I was at the mercy of the fighters and their ability to knock out other fighters.

I would sit in the studio with a ripe striper on my lap rooting for a quick kayo. It didn't matter by whom.

I wasn't paid for the show either. But I didn't lose anything. Television exposure never hurt my tackle sales.

The lack of pay and time wasn't the point anyway. The idea was to give Russo a chance to see how I came across the picture tube so he could judge for himself. He also wanted to check audience reaction.

Nick got his audience reaction, all right—but not in the way he expected. The station cancelled the show after a couple of months. It was the old blessing in disguise, another one of those lucky breaks I've had so often in my life. The station was flooded by more than 5,000 protest letters within a week.

That was all the reaction Nick wanted. He quit his job and took out a personal loan for $25,000. Then we went into hock to a Boston bank for another $100,000.

Gadabout Gaddis Productions was born.

The first order of business was to get some shows on film—color film, something we had decided upon long before. I fished rivers and lakes from Maine to Colorado to Florida, and we shot 13 episodes, enough for a fall or spring season.

When we finished, Nick started knocking on television station doors from coast to coast. Boston may have loved me, but the rest of the country was reluctant to even begin a courtship. But Nick is a very persistent cuss and managed to sell the show to KTRK-TV, Houston; WTAR-TV, Norfolk; WHEN-TV, Syracuse; WRGB-TV, Schenectady; and WHDH-TV, Boston.

Yes, sir, you read it right: my old pals, WHDH-TV.

Something had to give the second time around with that Boston station. It should have been an omen right there.

Whatever it was, another one of those big breaks was sitting right around the corner.

42. *Coast to Coast*

ONE MORNING NICK RUSSO GOT A TELEPHONE CALL AT OUR offices in Boston's Statler Office Building.

It was from a gentleman named Winston Mergott. Mergott is an avid fisherman. When he's not fishing, he is senior vice-president and general manager of Liberty Mutual Insurance Company.

"I'm having some friends from out of town staying with me for the weekend," he said. "I enjoy the show tremendously on Channel 5. These people are fishing buffs and I know they would too. Is it possible to borrow a few prints to show on my home projector?"

Mister, it sure was. We weren't about to tempt the wrath of a solitary fan.

Well, sir, that's when things started popping—I mean *really* popping!

Mergott's offices are only a block from ours. Winston himself returned the films the next week. He was more than carrying out an errand though. He had an idea.

Besides being a fishing nut, Winston is also a very cool business customer. He had already done some research and found out that there were 60 million fishing addicts in this country besides himself, 44 million of them licensed, according to the American Fishing Tackle Manufacturers Association. He also discovered that there were 22 million bowlers and 7 million golfers.

"Golf and bowling interests are well served by television," Mergott said. "And those shows are proven solid audience-getters. What about the poor fisherman?"

Nick nodded.

"What you're getting at is that you can get a tennis or golf pro," he said. "But where can you get a fishing pro?"

"Exactly," said Mergott. "I want to give fishermen that pro. And that pro is Gad. I think your series may be precisely the advertising vehicle our company is looking for."

That's when Nick must have had an impulse to get up and lock the door. But he didn't have to worry. As Mergott left, he promised, "I intend doing something about this."

And Winston did, despite some stiff opposition. Liberty Mutual's advertising department and advertising agency weren't enthused over his idea. But Mergott insisted that the show be given a test run.

He was given one, deliberately loaded against the show—exactly the way we all wanted it. It was run 13 weeks in fall, 1963, on New York City's WOR-TV, whose audience didn't figure to be exactly a hotbed of fishing enthusiasm. Also, the New York–New Jersey area is the most competitive market in the world for both TV and insurance.

The idea was that if the show could produce against that kind of a stacked deck, it would succeed anywhere.

To help gauge listenership, we dusted off the old $1 lure offer and announced it on the last four of the 13 shows. The results: 8,600 replied to the lure offer, another 1,000 wrote complimentary letters and many, many asked for a Liberty Mutual salesman to call on them.

There were a lot more figures and box scores that I won't

bore you with. But they all added up to one thing: the show had passed the acid test.

We were in!

We signed a five-year contract and Liberty Mutual put the show into 50 markets from coast to coast.

I retired from the tackle company after thirty-five years and concentrated on filming more shows for the series.

Today things are still buzzing. Between Liberty Mutual and various other sponsors, the show is now carried by 73 stations and blankets about 80 percent of the country. The rating people tell me I'm seen by twenty million people every week.

Well, sir, that's how it happened—as simple and confounded as that.

I'm just cocky enough to feel the show might have been a success whether Liberty Mutual had come along or not. But there's no getting around the job Winston Mergott did. Here's a man who believed in me so much that he went out and fought his own people to prove it.

How can I help but be grateful to a fellow like that?

Yet I treat that gentleman something terrible.

Every time I invite him fishing it rains cats and dogs. It's getting to be almost a joke between us. Once we hit a squall off the Cape, and I thought we'd be bailing out that boat till this day.

But that isn't the worst part.

When the weather hangs us up somewhere, more often than not we end up playing a little poker. And you can guess who wins.

I'll nick him for 65 cents here, a buck there.

That's gratitude, huh?

It just goes to show what kind of a so-and-so I really am.

43. *My Television Philosophy*

LET'S GET SOMETHING CLEAR: I'M NO EXPERT.

I never have been and I never will be.

I am just an average fisherman who builds pictures for the average fisherman. That's why I steer clear of expensive resorts while filming. I go only where the typical angler can afford to go. And that's why I use tackle that can be bought for less than $50. I don't want any advantages the run-of-the-mill fisherman doesn't have.

If our show has anything approaching what might be called a philosophy, that's it: unpretentious simplicity.

Above all my series is believable. It has to be. I film what happens. If I come up dry and don't catch a fish, that's what we show. If I get hung up on a tree, you'll see it. And if I slip on a rock, you'll see that too.

You will see it all because that's exactly what happened— and because that's what happens to the normal fisherman. I'm no different from the others—just a gent with his share of good and bad luck.

Every man who's ever baited a hook has known days when he couldn't catch a cold. Most have fallen down at one time or another. And just as many know what it's like to get hung up in a tree, or get a real backlash.

People watch these things happen to me on television, laugh, and say to themselves: "I guess I'm not the only darn fool who's had that happen to him."

As they say in those psychology books, the average Joe can identify with me. I reflect him. He looks into his TV screen and it becomes a mirror. He's watching me but seeing himself. And he enjoys that. He also sees I'm human.

It didn't take any particular genius to come up with this approach. It's just pure and simple common sense.

Yet, oddly, nobody ever thought this type of picture would interest the public. Before I hooked up with Nick Russo, I had plenty of people from the name networks and agencies tell me it wouldn't work.

"Gad," they'd say, "you can't show a picture like that. You can't show somebody catching a small, legal fish and have people enjoy it."

When I asked why not, they'd answer, "You just can't, that's all. Nobody will buy it."

Well, Nick and I believed in the approach. So we hocked our shirts and went ahead and did it anyway. And it clicked. It caught on where some past fishing shows featuring experts came up empty.

I'll tell you why I think they failed.

Some of these shows included fabulous pictures. You know, fantastic catches made in fantastic places. I have no quarrel with that. They're nice pictures to look at, and I enjoyed many

122

of them. Perfection is wonderful—if you can afford to be a perfectionist.

But that's just the point: only a small percentage of those who watch can. I'd say only about 80 percent of the 60 million people who fish in this country could afford it anyway. Joe Doakes could never make trips like those. And he could never afford to take the time it takes to line up these incredible catches.

Why should I misrepresent myself and my sponsors by hauling a 15-pound fish out of a stream where only one man in 20,000 could ever do it? It doesn't work that way. Sure you can catch one that big, but it may take you all season to do it.

If the average fish taken out of a particular stream is three or four pounds, that's what I take. I'm not going to sit around for a month just to get a freak catch. I could, but I won't. The average man can't sit around there for all that time, so why should I?

I want people to be able to watch me using things they can use and doing things they can do—not things they can't.

That's another place where those expert shows ran afoul. If anything, they discouraged the ordinary fisherman. If he believed those exceptional catches, he'd sit back and say: "I never had a catch like that. What kind of a dope am I?" A man can take only so much of that frustration before he'll lose interest and change to another channel in disgust.

Well, I don't go for it either. I'm no dope and neither is the average fisherman.

So that's another reason I show the people exact happens—nothing more, nothing less. And I absolutely to use any gimmicks or engage in even the mildest dec Who needs it?

And, as I've said, the average man can afford my k fishing. Fishing doesn't have to cost you a fortune. It d if you know how to pick your equipment and select your

There are all sorts of tackle on the market, good, some not so good. There are some $25 and $35 fly I wouldn't want to use. There are others in that price ra that are as fine as you'll ever find anywhere. You don't h to spend a lot of money for a rod, reel or anything else as l as you know what to look for.

The same goes for locations.

There's nothing wrong with expensive, fancy fishing resort Most of them are mighty fine places. I go to one every nov and then. I won't go to one to do a show because I don't believe in that. When I go it's for a vacation, to enjoy a little luxury along with the fishing. Some people go to Miami Beach or Acapulco or Bermuda to relax. I go to a fishing resort.

Let me tell you something about these places. They generally have a little better fishing than average. After all, if somebody sinks a million dollars into developing a place like that, he's usually going to make darn sure he builds it around a pretty fair fishing hole. On the other hand, I've seen a few that boast good fishing when it's only poor to fair.

What I'm trying to get across is this: resort fishing is fine as long as you understand what you're paying big money for—luxury and surroundings. It's not necessarily for better fishing than you can find along any free stream or lake.

While I'm on the subject, I'd like to get something else straight.

Plenty of people think a lot of places are resorts that really aren't. I mean there are a lot of camps and marinas from coast to coast that aren't expensive at all. They don't cost a person any more than staying anywhere else. And if you know something about fishing, you don't need to hire a guide at these places.

Just because a place has a fancy sign out front doesn't mean it costs an arm and a leg to get in. Of course, a few may be clip joints. It's like anything else in fishing—or in life, I guess: you have to pick your spots. And if you ask some simple questions in advance you usually won't get burned.

For the fun of it someday, inquire about the cost of one of these places. You may be pleasantly surprised. One thing for sure: you'll never know unless you ask.

So whether you use one of these moderately priced places or not, my point is a man doesn't have to spend a lot of money to fish a good spot. He can go almost anywhere and find all the fishing he wants, for there are thousands of miles of free fishing streams in this country.

And that's one of the keys to the success of family camping, which is becoming the biggest thing in the world. A man is going to empty his wallet in a hurry if he takes his wife and two kids on a cross-country vacation staying at fancy motels. But by camping, they can travel coast to coast, fishing the best streams as they go, for very little money—and have a barrel of fun while doing it.

So what I'm trying to emphasize is that you don't have to spend a fortune for good equipment or good location.

Another basic fact I stick to is that I refuse to set myself up as an expert.

Let me tell you something about so-called experts. I've fished with a lot of them, and most are no different from you and me. Oh, they may know a lot of fancy Latin words and terms that we don't understand. But a man catches fish with flies not words, and I'm too busy fishing to take time out to learn a lot of terminology.

Now I don't mean you can't learn something from these people. Naturally some anglers have more knowledge and experience in some areas of the sport than other fishermen. So they may have some information that may be of help if it fits in with your style.

I think this business of some people passing themselves off as be-all and end-all authorities on fishing is overdone.

So I refuse to preach how to do things on the show. I merely show how I do this or that and pass on methods that have worked for me. But I don't tell people to do it my way, that it's the only way or even the best way. I just do it and it's there if anyone wants to take it away with him.

Heck, I'd be an awful fool and a phony if I did say mine was the only way or the best way.

There are many ways to do most things in fishing. And a man uses those tacks which work for him. I do things my way because I've had pretty good luck using them over the years. But another man may use completely different methods and be successful too.

So who am I to say? And that's exactly the point: I don't.

Besides, no man knows all the answers about every type of fishing. Man, that's impossible.

I remember when I had question-and-answer sessions during those in-person shows I used to do. Some fellow would pop up and try to trap me on a question about a certain type of fishing—on nymphs, for example. Now he'd probably spent his life making a study of nymphs and knew his business inside out. Nymph fishing is tedious and a science in itself. I generally use nymph, but I'm not outstanding at it.

Well, sir, this fellow would give me a very technical question about it. My answer would always be simple. I'd just tell him I didn't know.

If I don't know an answer I'll just tell you so. And there is plenty, plenty I don't know. I'm learning every day. And any man who says he doesn't is either a fool or a liar.

A fisherman learns the sport the hard way, by doing it himself. Reading books and watching television is good, because he can pick up things. But he has to do it himself. And I mean everyone.

There is no man ever born who in one day could decide to become a fisherman, buy a complete outfit, and take off down a river and dry or wet fly big catches from the start. He's got to start from scratch, make plenty of mistakes and keep learning year after year after year.

I've heard of a few people who started out blind and accidentally caught a few big ones right off the bat. And, brother, let me tell you it's the worst thing that could have happened to them.

It's like some banjo-hitting rookie in baseball who clouts a home run in his first major league at-bat. He's all but ruined because all of a sudden he's got the feeling of power. You can't tell him a thing. He thinks he knows all the answers, but he really hasn't even gotten his feet wet yet.

It's the same in fishing, and the man can be spoiled for life.

It's far better if he isn't so lucky at first, learns through error, and comes to appreciate the sweat that goes into making a real catch. Practical experience is the best teacher: a man learns as he fishes. In addition he reads, watches and talks to other fishermen along the way to increase his knowledge. But basically he learns for himself, wasting a lot of time and maybe some money until he gets wise.

He buys different leaders, different flies and finally discovers he has to have a certain leader to get a certain fish; learns which fish go for a light leader, which go for a heavy leader, and what fish goes for what number fly. He probably buys a couple of dozen flies, and all are one size. He needs a No. 10 to catch a certain fish, but all he has are No. 8s. Well, it's painful and a little costly, but he learns.

Experience—there's nothing like it. And there's no way to avoid it. I went through it. I'm still going through it. And I want to continue going through it. The day I think I know it all is the day I quit, brother.

And the day I start experting or faking my shows is the day I'll quit television.

44. *How We Film Our Show*

A SCUBA DIVER PLUNGED INTO THE ICY KENNEBEC AND circled under my boat, grabbing the tow rope to act as a human anchor.

A director was perched above on a bridge, issuing more orders than Dwight Eisenhower did on D-Day, 1944.

A small army of technicians and cameramen—flown more than 400 miles from New York City to Hinckley, Maine—jumped at every command.

Men from an advertising agency fussed and fretted on shore.

Generators, sound boom and reflectors were positioned and repositioned.

Assistants held up "idiot cards" so I could read a prepared spiel.

And me, I just sat. Mister, I was plain bored and uncomfortable. It isn't easy sitting for hours in a boat without a line in the water.

Finally everything seemed set.

"Now," the director ordered me from above, "catch a fish!"

Well, sir, I just collapsed in that boat, my belly shook, and I laughed like to wake up the dead.

I doubt that the director, his crew or those agency boys appreciated the humor. But neither did they appreciate the fine art of fishing.

"Now, catch a fish!"—can you beat that?

That was the first and last time we ever tried to produce a commercial Hollywood-style.

That's all it was intended to be—a one-minute promo plugging our television series. It wouldn't have made any difference even if it had been just a 10-second spot. I just can't act. For better or worse, I have to do things naturally.

The same thing goes for reading a script. I can't do it.

Once we tried to do another of these one-minute promos in a New York studio with me reading from teleprompters. In fact it was just after that circus up in Hinckley. Those agency people don't quit easily. That flopped too.

I ended up ad libbing—the same way I ad lib the regular show.

Oh, I can read lines all right, I guess. But it's much more effective when anyone says what comes to mind naturally: spontaneous, off the cuff. And it's more in keeping with the casual tone of the show.

All this has been a long way of leading into what I want to explain: how we put together our television episodes.

Basically the filming is a simple operation centered around two men—the cameraman and me. That's all the traveling party we have. John Danyo has done most of the filming. We pack our gear into the rear of the Cherokee and hop around the country. We hire extra men when we get to where we want to do the filming. How many we need depends on where and how I fish. It may be three men, it may be five or six.

Locating help isn't a problem. We just get hold of a warden at the local fish and game department, the mayor, the chief of police or someone like that and tell him what we need. He puts us in touch with the right people in town.

Everyone has always been wonderfully cooperative and very helpful.

That goes along with something I learned long ago when I first began gaddin' about. Just level with people, tell them the truth and don't lie; and by golly they're willing to do anything in the world for you.

You'll find an exception here or there. But the lopsided majority are basically honest and helpful. It's human nature.

Now you may be sitting back and telling yourself: "Who's that Gad trying to fool? The reason he gets such great cooperation around the country is because he's on television. People help him because they want publicity for themselves or for their town."

Well, sir, I can't agree with that. I see the point you're trying to make all right. But I don't believe it. I think you'd get the same cooperation if you asked for it and didn't try to kid anybody. I was no TV personality back when I was riding the rails from coast to coast without a dime in the early days, and I was helped plenty.

People are hospitable by nature. The more you travel and meet people, the more you realize it.

So, as I was saying, the number of helpers we hire varies. Usually we need three men to handle our boats—one for mine, two for the cameraman's. The photographer needs two because he has to move quicker to catch certain angles, take advantage of the moving sun, and such. And two men can push his boat faster than one. We also often need a couple of extra hands to carry the equipment if we're going in off the beaten path a distance.

The whole operation takes a lot of teamwork.

The cameraman and I are always talking to the boys handling our boats, giving them instructions. John will be telling his lads to go here, go there. And when I've hooked a fish I'll be telling mine to pull to the left and keep the boat at a right angle to the camera at all times.

These youngsters usually catch on quickly to make our work a lot easier.

This teamwork pays off in better pictures—especially in capturing good strikes and jumps.

Often I can call the shot. Many times you can tell when a fish is going to jump by what the line is doing when he's coming up. So I'll say, "I think one's ready to jump, John. Start shooting." He'll begin grinding and we end up with some interesting pictures.

In all, we shoot quite a bit of film. There are 947 feet in a finished show, and we generally take about four feet for every one foot used.

It takes anywhere from a day to a week to film one half-hour show. The time differs for many reasons. We may run into a streak where it rains for days. There may be equipment problems. There can be a hundred reasons for a delay.

We've wrapped up a picture in one day.

I recall one we did going for kingfish in the Gulf of Mexico off Freeport, Texas. We arrived one morning at daybreak and by eight o'clock had made all the arrangements, found a location and were anchored. It turned out we were sitting on top of a school of kingfish and they began hitting, brother. Every time I threw out bait I got a fish pronto. And all of them were from 10 to 36 pounds.

It doesn't take long to make a film like that.

We got all the fish we wanted in no time. So we started shooting odds and ends on the boat and scenery, ate lunch and were back on the dock by three in the afternoon with a pretty fair picture.

I've shot other shows in a day too—like the silver salmon picture we did on the Columbia River near Ilwaco, Oregon.

Like anything else in fishing, you've got to be lucky to

wrap up a show in a day. Where there was no luck, I've spent a week.

Now I'm not talking about staying a week in a place just to catch a fish. If I don't get one, that's okay. It doesn't embarrass me any more than it does to fall in a stream or get a line hooked on a bush. All these things happen to fishermen every day, so why should they bother me? I'm no magician and don't pretend to be.

If I don't catch a fish, we'll just show me coming up empty. It's as simple as that. In fact some of my shows that have shown me coming up empty have drawn the biggest number of letters.

I remember one episode we did on Upper Thomas Lake in Colorado, about 11,500 feet up on Snowmass Peak. It's a fabulous lake with plenty of nice trout.

We filmed our trip up the rugged mountainside by Jeep, and that was tremendous in itself. When we got there I waded out to just above my knees. I wouldn't go farther because there were plenty of rocks, and dead ahead the water was very clear as it obviously dropped. I've been told it's 90 feet deep in spots there.

Meanwhile, I saw plenty of fat trout, but they weren't buying anything I had to sell. I changed lures constantly, but those sulky rainbows weren't interested in any of them. I didn't get a strike all afternoon.

Okay. No problem.

We had a leisurely dinner by campfire and headed back down the treacherous, beautiful mountainside—and filmed it all. I'll never forget looking down across miles and miles of valley, with one lonely steer grazing there as the sun began to set.

It was a portrait—a living portrait.

And that's how we faded out the episode.

So I had no fish. So what? To me this whole big picture—being aware of all the many worlds going on around a fisherman—is part of what makes our sport so great. If I've had a chance to soak up some of this world's nature and scenery, I've had a good time right there—fish or no fish.

And apparently a lot of people agree. That show drew a ton of mail.

What I'm getting at is that you won't catch me hanging around a place until I can get a big fish to make myself look good on television.

What I'm talking about when I say I've spent a week in a place is being hung up because of weather or something. You can show a picture of failing to get a fish. But you've got to show something. You can't, though, if there's no sun or some piece of equipment is on the blink or the like.

Once I spent close to a week in Missoula, Montana, and still didn't get a foot of film out of it.

That happened right after I'd almost been hung up for good on the Salmon River in eastern Idaho, a story I'll get to in a later chapter. But some of our equipment had been lost, some ruined in that accident and John had hopped a plane back to Hollywood to get new gear.

I went ahead to Missoula, where we were due to film next, to wait for him. I knew it would take John about three days to get back. To pass the time I asked some of the boys at a local sporting goods store where I could fish nearby.

The Bitterroot is very close to Missoula, but they suggested I go south on that river to a little place called Lolo. I believe that's where Lewis and Clark met the Blackfoot Indians during the famous exploring expedition of the Far West in the early 1800s.

Well, sir, it turned out to be one heck of a tip.

As soon as I hit Lolo, I could see the fish rising—nice rainbows. I assembled a rod, put on a dry fly and got my body out there in a hurry. And, by golly, I hit three rainbows in no time—one two pounds, one three pounds and one close to four pounds. They were beautiful fish—some of the best I'd taken in weeks.

For three days I fished that spot and for three days I had wonderful luck and a wonderful time.

John arrived on the third night. I filled him in on this fabulous place as we ate dinner. I mean I was like a little kid on the night before Christmas. I couldn't wait for morning to get some of this fantastic fishing on film.

It turned out I couldn't sleep for another reason that night. Man, it thundered something fierce. Then the rains came—and stayed. After two days of it we had to leave. We were scheduled to begin shooting somewhere else. Even if we'd stayed until the rain had stopped (it may still be pouring there for all I know), it wouldn't have done any good. The river had already swelled about two and a half feet.

So sometimes nothing goes right.

Usually, though, it's not so bad at all and my typical day on location is simple.

I'm up at six o'clock and by eight I've showered, shaved, dressed and have some breakfast. It doesn't do any good to get going any earlier because you have to wait until the sun is high to get the proper lighting for quality filming.

We usually begin shooting an hour or so later, depending on how long it takes to get to actual location. Then I get into my waders, tie on a fly and get into the stream. By now the sun is in its proper position and we're ready to start filming.

We normally stay out until about four in the afternoon. There's still about four hours of mighty fine fishing left, but we can't take advantage of it. Once the sun starts fading into the west and ducking behind a hill, we have to quit shooting because there isn't enough quality light.

Often I can't stand the temptation, though, and send the cameraman back to the lodge while I stay out and fish for the fun of it. It's a sin to let all that good fishing go to waste.

And that's that—a typical day on location.

You may have noticed I mentioned sending the cameraman back to the lodge. We generally stay at lodges or ranches while on location. I believe in comfort when possible. Camping doesn't excite me—it really never has—and I keep it to a minimum. I'll do it when I have to: when we go into real rugged back country or when I'm with friends who want to do it. But that doesn't mean I have to like it.

Cooking? Yes, I get a kick out of that, although I wouldn't want to make it a habit either. I can take care of myself around a stove though. And I do more than a normal share of being chef because I'm not always satisfied with restaurant food.

The whole food picture is changing in this country. Everything comes from a can today. The result is that the days of really good eating are pretty much past. Naturally there are exceptions—a rare restaurant here and there. But generally speaking prepared food has become so synthetic that I don't even want to bother with it much.

I believe you can put almost anything in front of the

132

younger generation and they'll eat it. Don't blame them. They don't know any better.

But don't try it with me.

You don't have to go any further than the first thing I put in my stomach in the morning: orange juice. I'm a nut on orange juice—*fresh orange juice*. I have to have a big tumblerful first thing every morning. Have you tried to get a glass of fresh orange juice in a restaurant lately? Walk into most any place from coast to coast and they don't know what you're talking about. I mean it.

Like I say, everything comes from a can. But I won't settle for that condensed excuse for fresh juice and usually I eventually get what I want. I may end up waiting a half-hour and paying $1.25 for it, but I get it. It's just something I must have.

I mention orange juice, but you can go down the menu, item by item. Carelessly prepared food and synthetics drive me frantic. That's why I end up cooking for myself more than I'd prefer to.

I love a good broiled medium-rare steak with broccoli, creamed corn and a little wild rice or potato on the side.

Fixing potatoes is my specialty. I take a raw spud and slice it normally for frying. I get a good iron skillet, put in plenty of non-fat oil and get it smoking good. Then I work the potato in and out of the pan fast. The slices are nice and brown with a slight raw taste still in them.

Give me a mug of strong black coffee and maybe a slice of homemade bread to top it all off and I'm a king.

Fish? I like to eat it once in a while, but not too often. Trout is over-rated. Mackerel and bluefish are too oily for me. My favorite is scrod—pan-fried scrod. I love it.

In fact, when the food is right, I love to eat—period. Like a lot of us, though, I have to discipline my eating habits—going light on two favorites especially: bread and potato.

I used to be a big eater until about five years ago. My weight got as high as 197 pounds and I said enough. That's too much on a 5-7½ frame. No doctor had to tell me. I knew it myself and made it my business to lose 30 pounds in a hurry.

So now I weigh 165 and intend to keep it there.

I guess a lot of people are surprised when they meet me. They tell me I look a lot bigger on television. And I suppose

I do. All the gear—especially the fishing jacket and waders —tend to puff a man out of proportion.

So far I've told only about the easiest part in making the series: filming. There's also a less glamorous side behind the scenes: production. It takes plenty of hard work by between 20 and 30 people to make the show what it is. All these experts—editors, specialists, lab people and all—pool their efforts for about two months between the time I film the action and the time the final product is ready for showing on television.

And all that hard work is done in good old Hollywood, U.S.A.

First, all the film—nearly three-quarters of a mile of it —is developed and processed.

Then an editor plows through all that footage and whittles it down to what we'll need for the half-hour show.

Then I tackle the edited film twice. The first time is to make sure the scenes flow in the right order. The second time is to re-acquaint myself with the subject matter, since often it's been a month or so since I did the filming.

Finally I'm ready to narrate the voice track. I watch the film on a big studio screen and ad lib the action taking place.

Sometimes a problem will develop while I'm narrating. A technical difficulty will crop up or I'll flub a line. So we'll have to start again. Well, sir, my narration will be different just as many times as I have to re-do it. With my style of ad libbing, I couldn't do it the same if I tried to. The facts remain the same, but that's about all.

Next come the sound effects. A specialist runs through the film and picks out which sounds he'll have to re-create— a fish splashing, a boat motor perking, a bird chirping. Once we showed a cannon roaring and he had to go out and search up an appropriate boom for that too.

The music man takes over next. He runs through the film and decides which mood of background music best suits that episode.

Once the effects and music people have dug up their material and recorded it, the operation really gets tricky. There are now three separate sound tracks: narration, sound effects and music. They must be blended into one track that matches the film to the split-second.

Finally one composite is made called the "answer print."

That's when we know, after about six weeks, what we really have—or don't have. From this we make any final corrections, including true color adjustment—if need be making the blues bluer, the greens greener and so forth.

Once all this is checked out we're ready for the final step: slapping the title and credits on the show's fore and aft.

Finally, we have a product ready for the can and distribution to your favorite television station.

It's a fascinating education watching these men work backstage; I never cease to be amazed by their talent and ingenuity. And no one is more fascinating than their boss, Gordon Zahler. Now there's a man for you, mister. He's really something—a fabulous character. He's brilliant and imaginative—and no quitter.

Gordon was seriously injured as the result of a fall in a Hollywood high school gymnasium when he was 14. The accident left him a paraplegic of the most severe type. He can move only his head and can't even smoke a cigarette without help. Instead of retreating into a shell and feeling sorry for himself, Gordon has become one of the most successful men in Hollywood. He has his own business, General Music Corporation, which has done effects for numerous motion pictures and several hundred TV shows, including the *Woody Woodpecker* series.

If you want inspiration and a lesson in life, Gordon Zahler is it. He is a marvel.

And so is his entire operation. Not only am I amazed by it, but I'm thankful for it.

Without these boys and their ability, Gadabout Gaddis The Flying Fisherman wouldn't be what it is today.

45. TV Isn't All Fun

FISHING FOR TELEVISION ISN'T ALL FUN.

Now don't misunderstand me. I thoroughly enjoy doing the series and consider myself a lucky, lucky man to be able to fish and travel the way I do and get paid for it. But there are some trying, not-so-glamorous moments that provide a few minuses to go along with all the pluses.

We had an experience not long ago in eastern Idaho, near the Montana border, that points up what I mean.

The idea was to film a float trip from Challis to a bridge about eight miles downstream on the west branch of the Salmon River as I fished for rainbow, browns and cutthroat.

Now let me tell you something, mister; that west Salmon is a wild, wild river. The current is fast and furious. And making it even more infernal the day we were on it was that it was running about a foot above normal.

As I've said, we usually use two boats when filming—one for me, one for the cameraman. But because of the conditions and the type of film we wanted to make, we decided to use just one on the Salmon: a new 10-man rubber raft. And four of us climbed aboard—John Danyo, myself and two strong, young paddlers.

We photographed some of the eye-catching scenery as we traveled downstream, and stopped from time to time at gravel bars where I'd get out and wade and fly fish. We'd drift and cast, drift and cast. It was working out beautifully.

Then two things happened which should have been tip-offs, a couple of sweet omens if I ever saw one.

First it began to cloud up. So we started to hurry the trip a bit. If we got caught in the rain up there, it would be too bad for our big expensive cameras. We hadn't brought along covers.

Then I hooked a big trout, and I mean a real granddaddy. The camera was grinding away and I was having a ball. But I let him get in among some roots along shore and lost him. That fish was a lot smarter than me for more reasons than one. If I had known what was going to happen around the next corner, I'd have headed for shore too.

We continued downstream. There was a big bend to the left about three miles before the bridge. As we made the turn we saw an enormous cottonwood tree down and sprawled more than halfway across the river. It must have fallen only a day or two before and loomed dead ahead.

We were in for trouble and knew it.

The current was so furious and the tree upon us so fast that we couldn't avoid it. We hit it—and immediately swamped.

The raft wedged between two big heavy lower limbs. I

136

reached for a limb on top and swung up onto it. John was holding the camera over his head. I grabbed it so he could swing himself up. I had to be careful to get hold of it in just the right way so the magazine wouldn't fall out.

Then the boys scrambled up. So everybody had gotten out of the water and we were tremendously lucky. But we had lost a lot of gear, two film magazines worth $150 each, expensive batteries, a light meter, several thousand feet of unused film and a lot of priceless film already shot.

And there we were, like four wet monkeys in a tree with no place to go.

It got a little scary.

The rubber raft was swamped but not sunk. It wasn't any good to us though, because it couldn't be budged from the fork in the tree against such a savage current.

An apparent alternative was that the tree trunk extended back to shore. But that wasn't much good either because, right next to us, it dipped about eight inches below water until the trunk thickened near shore.

So we sat where we were for five hours—count 'em, mister: five hours! Ever sit in a tree for five hours with a murderous river surging beneath?

We weren't exactly idle though. All the time we were scheming and trying to do things to escape. No matter how we figured it though, the only route was across the tree. The riddle was how. With the powerful current sweeping over most of the trunk, it seemed impossible to manage. One of the young fellows tried it several times. But each time he put a foot down, the current would sweep it off.

Finally he took some quarter-inch rope that had been attached to the raft and swung it until he lassoed a tree on shore next to the one that had fallen. He put a lot of pressure on the line, pulling it real taut, before he knotted it to a thick branch on our end.

What he had done was to create a guy line across the mostly submerged tree trunk to make a sort of rope railing over the path to safety. Then this kid took one heck of a chance. Remember now, this current was churning furiously and he could easily be swept underneath. And if that happened he was just about a sure goner—either swept downstream or caught in the branches below. Either way he'd be a drowned man.

The youngster said he wasn't worried, but he had to be.

Finally the boy got both feet on the trunk. Then he grasped the guide line and started inching his way toward shore. When he got close enough to another tree jutting out from land, he made a mighty lunge for it—and made it!

Well, sir, that left one down and three to go.

No sooner had that boy scrambled ashore than we heard somebody laughing up a storm.

Floating downstream was a little rubber raft with a game warden aboard.

"Trouble, boys?" he cackled.

"Laugh!" we roared. "Go ahead and laugh!"

The warden lent us a paddle and each man in turn used it as a sort of wading staff to follow the first boy, keeping the rope line underarm as we went.

Now to get some help. One of the boys said he'd try to find a house where he could borrow an axe. The idea was to cut the lower branches and free the raft. So off he went.

An hour later he was still gone. I was getting more than a little anxious, so I took off after him.

I had taken off my leather boots—they had been soaked like everything else and darned if I could get my feet back into them. But I went barefoot anyway, and walked and walked and walked some more. I waded through two streams, hiked across a field about an eighth of a mile wide with lots of willows, and plodded through a big area of swampland where the mud came up to my knees.

Just then I met the man coming back and, hallelujah: he had the axe. I told him to go ahead back and I'd follow. You can see what a big help I was all along.

My main concern now was the boots I'd been carrying all the while. I was afraid they'd shrink. So I washed my feet in some water, let them dry in the sun and finally worked them back into the boots without socks. In fact I left the boots on until 11 o'clock that night so they'd dry out properly and not lose their size and shape.

I finally made it back to the fallen tree, we got the lower limb cut, and freed the raft.

A little later we reached the bridge. It was almost dark and we were about ten hours behind schedule. But I'll tell you: it sure was better late than never—something I had given more than a little thought to.

It had been a costly trip and a frightening one. But I

had no complaints. Everyone was safe, and a man can't ask for more than that.

A postscript to the story is that we were able to salvage only a small sequence of fishing on a sandbar in the Salmon River. When we opened the camera we found that water had seeped into that one precious magazine we had been so careful to rescue.

I would have loved trying the whole thing again the next day, but we couldn't. We were due on location in Missoula, Montana, the next day. Besides, John had to hop a plane for Hollywood to get all new equipment.

But I'll promise you one thing, brother: I'll get back to that west branch of the Salmon one of these days. And even if I get dunked again, I hope we can keep the film dry so you can see it.

46.   Fishermen Are Characters

FISHERMEN ARE CHARACTERS.

They have more idiosyncrasies than a mother alligator has babies.

The one that amuses me most is the compulsion to go a long way off to fish. If you don't believe me, watch the comedy that takes place every day in any fishing camp in the country. A camp may have 150 boats for rent, and by 7 o'clock on a weekend morning they're gone. By 7:30 there isn't a boat in sight.

Where are they?

Everyone is way down the stream or scattered around the lake. Not a one hung around the dock. The irony of it is, I'll bet anyone 10-1 there's just as good fishing by the dock as anywhere else. Perhaps better, because there's no one else fishing there.

That's why I often start right by the dock.

But that's one of the quirks of fishing: it isn't fun when you're on top of it.

Take any body of water in the United States. Jim lives on the west end, Joe on the east end. Each bounces out of bed at daybreak, makes breakfast and jumps into his boat.

Jim dashes three miles to the east end to fish. Joe rushes three miles to the west end to drop his line.

I laugh at these things but I'm no different, really. Don't fool yourself, mister: I do the same things myself plenty, even though I know darn well I'm being silly.

An example of what I mean happened one day during World War II when I was giving those clinics for the Air Corps around Florida.

The Hillsboro River runs right through the heart of Tampa. It always has been good bass fishing, but for some reason Bob Grant and I used to go about 80 miles east to Lake Kissimmee to fish for the same thing.

One morning Bob was due to pick me up at 9 o'clock. Just before eight, another fellow I knew dropped by the house.

"Gad, I haven't had any fish for a long time," he said. "How about taking me out and catching me a couple of bass?"

I said sure, because I had time to spare before Bob was due.

We hopped into my boat and headed downstream maybe 100 yards. There were a lot of reeds there, a good place to drop a bug. In no time we had picked up six or seven bass, about two and a half pounds apiece.

We headed back to the house. Just as we crossed the yard, Bob pulled into the driveway. My wife was on the porch; she and Bob admired our string of fish.

Then Bob and I got into his car. My wife asked where we were going. When I told her Kissimmee, she blew her top. I mean you could have heard her clear down in Bradenton.

"You have all the fish in the world in your front yard, but you have to drive halfway across the state to go fishing!" she bellowed. And, brother, did she ever make an issue out of that. She was right, of course.

See what I mean? For some reason, fishing is no fun when you're on top of it.

Take the fishing lodge where I often stay in Bingham, Maine. The Kennebec River runs right by its front door. I could fly cast off the sun deck if I wanted to. Water's edge is less than 30 feet away. But do I? Heck no. More often than not I'll pile into the car and drive down the road a half-mile and fish off an island downstream a piece or up to a fork 20 miles upstream.

There's just something in human nature that makes a fisherman want to wander. I guess there's a little gadabout in all of us.

We're all a little daffy.

Take those fishing calendars. There are millions circulated every year, and they are read by fishermen from coast to coast. Read, I said—not necessarily believed.

The dates are colored to rate the fishing: green for good fishing, yellow for fair fishing, white for poor fishing. It's based on the phases of the moon or something. Fishermen are wild for these calendars.

When a fisherman goes fishing he checks the card and says, "Oh-oh, fishing's no good this week." But he goes anyway. He accidentally catches a few fish, so he goes around telling everyone in sight the calendar is a phony.

Then there's the other fisherman who checks the card and says, "Gee, it's green. Are we ever going to have luck today!" So he goes fishing and comes back empty. He tells everybody the card is useless.

But neither fellow will throw the calendar away. He always watches it—mostly to see if he can prove it wrong, I guess. That's a true fisherman for you.

And there are almost as many theories and philosophies in fishing as there are fishermen.

Some will get a catch in a certain spot and immediately take off for another area. They insist there are no more fish there or that none will bite there because they've been disturbed. Others will stay in the same spot till doomsday after they've made a catch there, and will keep going back day after day.

Well, sir, this is where I try to use my head a little and draw the line on the foolish habits we fishermen fall into. I mean I stop and try to analyze the situation a little bit.

First, am I fishing for migrating fish or non-migrating fish? If it's migrating fish in salt water, I won't go back to the same spot day after day. Heck, they're here now and 10 miles away in a couple of hours. Yet I know a lot of people on Cape Cod who keep going back to the same spot after they've caught a few striped bass there. They don't realize—or won't believe—that stripers continually migrate. Non-migrating fish are a different story. They're like people. They live in communities. They've got an underwater town here, another 8 miles away, and so on. They settle in an area because of food supply or the shape of the land or some such reason. Once a man finds these communities, he can score time and again if the fish are in the mood to bite. They're there.

Fishing isn't all luck. You have to study each situation. Lots of people see a body of water and to them it's just water. They don't try to visualize what's underneath. They don't study the contour of the land that tips off the lay of the land beneath.

For example, if there's a point of land jutting out into the water, that point will continue under water. And fish usually lay on that point.

You have to stop and figure these things out.

I know I'll get a lot of letters now, and people will tell me they don't pay attention to any of these ideas and still catch plenty of fish. All I can say is congratulations and good luck, people. Sure you'll get an occasional fish—usually one passing through, traveling from one community to another.

All I'm saying is that I play the percentages and go where the fish should be. I still get hung up on empty days, but I think I make out better going with the odds in the long run.

That happened to me the past year. I went out with a real good fisherman who was very familiar with the area we were fishing. We were going for cutthroat, and I caught a beauty out of a brush pile.

"Okay," said my friend, "let's go. That's all we're going to get here."

I didn't say anything and we moved. To make a long story short, this happened three times. Each time I got a catch we moved. Then I landed a fourth fish—a nice 4-pounder.

"Let's see if I can get another here," I said.

"No," he protested. "Once you get a fish in a spot you won't get another. They're all disturbed."

Well, sir, I spoke my piece and he finally agreed to let me try. I suppose he wanted to humor an old man. But you can guess what happened. I cracked his theory wide open by catching four more trout in a hurry. We moved and I did the same thing again.

Now that's all I can tell you. I did it. I don't know why. It wasn't that I was a better fisherman than this fellow. We just had different theories.

And so it goes: every angler to his own ideas, his own quirks.

Then there are the old wives' tales that still exist in fishing today.

Years ago people had the idea that when you grabbed hold of a fish, and your dry hand took some of that scum off him, that you were doing that fish harm. They felt that if you released that fish back into the water, fungus would grow where he had been wiped dry and that it would kill him.

Well, sir, that's been proven 100 percent wrong. Biologists will tell you that normal handling doesn't impair the health of a fish a bit. Yet a lot of people still won't believe it. And, brother, do I ever get mail on it! People see me handling fish before tossing them back and give me the dickens.

Look, friend. Go into any fish hatchery in the country and you'll see the brooders being handled constantly and never feeling any effect from it. Or look in on the many lakes where salmon are trapped and their eggs taken. These salmon are pawed plenty before being released and they aren't hurt in the slightest.

So you can handle a fish all you want. As long as you've hooked him in the mouth and don't squeeze him so hard that you injure his gills, that fish will be fine when he's tossed back. He'll just wonder what happened, that's all.

Thank heaven though there's one old tale that's disappearing from fishing.

Some people used to think you'd scare fish away if you talked in a boat. That's a lot of bunk. You can talk all you please. The only things in the world that will frighten a fish are when you cast a quick shadow over the water suddenly or bang the side of your boat on a rock.

If you stand up suddenly in a boat, your shadow jumps and the fish will jump too. Or if you bump an anchor on the side of the boat, the noise will often bother the fish. A metal anchor clanging off rocks on the bottom makes an awful racket, too, and will disturb the fish.

Both problems can be overcome fairly simply.

The quick shadow can be eliminated by just being a little careful. And anchors aren't the problem they used to be. Up until this past year I usually wrapped mine in canvas to help absorb the shock if it hit the boat or a rock. I tried foam rubber, but it wouldn't stay fixed.

Now there are beautiful rubber-coated anchors on the market. I saw one at a sportsman's show and the salesman sent me one. I can't do without it now. It's a great innovation.

143

Other than a quick shadow or a noisy anchor you won't disturb a fish. Certainly normal talking won't frighten him.

It used to be wonderful though. Fishermen would say, "Shhh, be quiet. I got a bite."

Well, that's exciting to a woman. Females get a big kick out of it. They're impressed by the drama of it, I guess. And, come to think of it, keep them thinking that way. It's a good way to keep them quiet in a boat anyway.

47. Some Mighty Strange Catches

EVERYTHING NIBBLING ON YOUR LINE ISN'T A FISH.

I've seen some mighty strange catches over the years.

Probably the weirdest of all came one night in Tampa Bay just after World War II. I still owned that 35-foot cruiser and occasionally chartered it out for fishing parties. I'd take groups out into the bay for tarpon, red fish, trout, snook and the like.

At night we'd often anchor with the outgoing or incoming tide by the Gandy Bridge. The tide would carry the bait toward the bridge. And with the bridge all lit up, tarpon would come in toward the bright lights, because the bait would gather there.

This particular night I had a bunch from a local garage, and these boys had gotten pretty well gassed before they met me at the pier. We drifted out by the bridge and got ready for some action. Most of these fellows had hand lines. But one had a boat rod with a heavy sinker, and was using pin fish for bait. Well, sir, he was having a little trouble casting. Finally he wound up and made as wild a cast as I've ever seen. His line went clear up on the bridge, and—bzzzz!

My Lord, he'd got a catch—a Greyhound bus!

He had hooked the little red night light on the top left side near the luggage rack. The bus was moving along pretty good and this boy's line was singing to beat the band. I mean it was really singing a tune.

Man, I want to tell you I've never seen a look on a fisherman's face quite like that one. Never in my life. I swear he thought he'd hooked a whale. And with that line humming, he

144

was holding onto that rod for dear life. Well, sir, the line finally busted, and the pop sounded like a rifle report.

The poor guy looked at me, really dazed, and said: "Gee, I lost him."

I darn near fell out of the boat. I'll never forget that as long as I live. It was that funny.

Oh, I've seen plenty of things on the end of a fishing line that shouldn't have been there. I've caught everything from swallows to alligators.

I hooked my first gator in late 1950. *Look* magazine was doing that feature story on ten of us from my tackle company as we tested equipment for more than a week in the Everglades' Shark River country. A five-foot alligator spotted my plug and swung right over to it. He hit it three times before he got hold of it. When I hit him hard, the hook slipped out of his mouth and caught near the tip of his tail.

Now you talk about a gator raising the devil. I finally got him in real close, right next to the boat, when the line snapped. All of which was okay with me.

I've got it all in a movie.

I have other films of reeling in a three-footer with a fly rod on the St. John's River in northeast Florida.

Let me tell you something about alligators. I respect them, but I don't fear them. If you can get hold of the tail with one hand, and get the other hand clamped over his mouth, you've got him licked. Now you're not going to do this to any 10-footer, because you could never control a tail that big or powerful. But if you could, just two fingers would lock his mouth as long as you had him by the "lips." His jaws are locked powerless. The same principle is true no matter what the gator's size. But don't let him get that mouth open or it's all over.

I've caught dozens of gators accidentally all over Florida. You won't ever hook one in the mouth, though. At least I never did. It's just about impossible. A gator's mouth is all bone, so there's nothing to sink a hook into. Instead you'll catch them on a scale, usually along the tail.

These alligators are something. They'll spot a plug a good way off and come a-running. And they're persistent. Like that first one I had in the Everglades, they keep coming no matter how many times they lose the plug. And if your line doesn't snap, you can bring him in.

I'll tell you something that scares me a lot more than an

alligator, though. It's those shypokes and herons you see in the swamps or on the shores of rivers and lakes. They can be murder. Those are the birds with long necks and pointed bills. You have to keep them at arm's distance because they're frightened and will fight. Watch out. The beak is like a dagger and will put your eye out. But if you hook one on a wing it's difficult to get him free and not have him close to you. So I'd rather snare a gator anytime.

I've accidentally caught plenty of other things too.

I have nailed many a sea gull on a casting plug. They'll spot it, dive like a kamikaze plane, and pluck it right out of the water.

I've come up with plenty of ducks too.

And swallows.

That's happened to me four or five times alone in Little French Creek on the St. Lawrence River in Clayton, New York. I'll spot a big bluegill, put on a fly and by golly on the backcast a swallow will swoop down and grab that fly in mid-air. There's no trouble though. I just bring him in and unhook him. He's all right. He just has a little sore jaw for awhile.

I'll tell you one critter that's a lot more trouble—a whole lot more trouble. That's the snake. Look out for him.

I remember once fly casting for bass along the shore of Lake Kissimmee in Florida. I was working my bug through some lily pads very slowly when I felt the line jump a bit. I immediately began reeling in.

I had a catch, all right—a five-foot moccasin snake. I'd hooked him in his thick, heavy body. I didn't see that venomous old boy until I had reeled him close to the boat.

When I saw what I had I nearly died.

There's a tendency to panic in such a situation. Luckily, I didn't. I just cut the leader and that customer took off—taking my brand new bug with him.

The big thing to remember when coming across a rattler or moccasin is to keep your boat as far away from him as possible without making a fuss. If he gets aboard, you might as well go over the side.

If a snake is swimming close by, keep quiet and let him alone. If you attempt to get closer for a better look, the odds are you'll scare him. And once frightened, he'll head for the nearest thing he sees—probably your boat.

He won't be out to hurt you. He'll merely be looking for a place to hide. But the result will be the same if he gets aboard.

And you'd be surprised how difficult it is to keep that snake out of a boat once he's put his mind to climbing in. He's fast and he's powerful and you can't flip him away with an oar. Don't fool yourself and think you can. If he manages to get in the boat, friend, you're on your own. That reptile is deadly.

You'd be amazed at the number of people who apparently don't think so. I know of fishermen who have actually tried to catch them with rod and reel.

Well, everyone to his own poison.

I guess I've been luckier than most men. I learned about snakes early from an expert on the matter—a Presbyterian minister, of all people.

Reverend John Largent, Jr., knows it all when it comes to those critters, and I suppose that isn't so irregular at that. Who should know better about serpents than a preacher?

The Reverend is a fabulous person. He has a congregation in Tampa now, but worked out of Palatka, Florida, when I knew him. Besides being an A-1 outdoorsman, he's an intelligent, all-around fellow who does wonderful work for his church. Yes, sir, John is quite a man.

He knows all about snakes because he grew up in the back country and worked his way through school hunting, trapping and fishing.

I've had dozens of snake experiences with John.

The scariest happened one night when we weren't even fishing.

"Come on, Gad," the preacher said. "Let's go frog hunting."

"Not me," I said. "I love frog legs, but I'm not going to prowl around those swamps barefooted like you to get them."

"Okay, so put on waders," he said. "Let's go."

I did and we did.

In no time at all John picked off five or six frogs. He'd just shine a light on them so they wouldn't jump and pick them off with his .22 pistol. I tagged along carrying a bag.

Well, sir, all of a sudden the Reverend spotted a big old bullfrog maybe ten feet away. But for some reason he didn't shoot and I couldn't understand it.

"Don't move, Gad," John whispered. "Just slowly shine your light down at my feet."

And there crawling across his bare feet was a deadly poisonous moccasin. Boy, I nearly passed out.

The Reverend didn't move a muscle and barely moved his

lips as he whispered, "If that devil makes me lose that big frog, I'll blow his head off!"

That's just the way he said it—cool and determined.

The old snake must have heard him because he stopped. But when he started to move again, the frog jumped.

Well, sir, John slipped a .45 from another holster and did just what he promised he'd do.

"Let's get out of here, preacher," I said.

"Aw, snakes won't hurt you as long as you know how to handle them," he said.

And he kept me wandering around that swamp half the night.

I have to hand it to the Reverend Mr. Largent though. He knows his business.

One time he and I were fishing a little spot called Turpentine Creek up off the Oklawaha River near Silver Springs, Florida. We were pulling in some nice bass when we came to a log jutting out about head-high over the water. And right on top was a big moccasin sunning himself.

I picked him off with my .22 pistol and we started to move our boat past the end of the log. All of a sudden John pulled the boat up short, backed it up a bit and then swung a wide arc around it. His hunch was a good one. The log was hollow, and right inside was another big moccasin. If we'd have kept going the way we had been, our faces would have been right next to that old boy—and you can imagine what would have happened.

Another time John and I were paddling through a creek where we had to squeeze our boat through a narrow passage between some thick bushes. And the lower branches were covered with wasp nests.

If you ever hit one of those nests, you'd better head over the side and into the water, because those wasps will be all over you like a squadron of dive bombers. I mean they'll swarm you and about sting you to death.

So we started to pass through this stretch with the care of a ship easing through a mine field.

Then we saw something else—snakes again. The whole area was crawling with them. And all kinds: moccasins, black snakes, water snakes, chicken snakes—you name it. Some bushes had six or eight of them clinging to them. Most were non-poisonous, but that didn't make us feel any more comfortable.

Between the wasps and the snakes, a man's impulse is to get out of there as fast as possible. But that's about the worst thing he can do. He's got to ease himself through to make sure he doesn't disturb the wasps.

And as careful as John was slipping us through, his oar blade came within a whisker of demolishing a nest. He caught the oar just in time and turned the blade over flat, and it just skimmed underneath the nest.

"How lucky can a guy be?" John sighed as we finally cleared the last bush.

"I'm just happy I'm with a man who lives right, preacher," I grinned.

"Come on," he laughed, kicking over the motor. "Let's get out of here."

Just give me all the distance you can between me and a snake when I'm in a boat.

One of my cameramen once wanted to get closer to a snake in water than a man should ever try. It happened while we were filming a show on Okeechobee. The Reverend was along on that trip, too, handling our boat.

We were passing through a gap about 50 feet wide when we saw a rattler swimming leisurely about 20 yards ahead. He was just coasting along with his head out of the water and his rattlers up.

Was he ever a big one! I'll give you my word he was six feet if he was an inch!

"Look-a-there!" the cameraman hollered.

"I see him," I said. "Leave him be."

"Let's get him on film," the photographer enthused. "He'd make a great picture."

I appreciated the cameraman's spirit and dedication. I knew it was a temptation. The snake *would* have made some interesting footage. And no one wants to make the most interesting picture possible more than I. At the same time a man has to be practical. After all, if I'm going to shoot the film, I'd just as soon be around to narrate it afterward. There's no sense being the bravest fisherman in the U.S.A. if you're also going to be the deadest. There's a time and place to be a hero. This just wasn't one of those times.

"C'mon," the photographer persisted.

"Hush!" I said. "You'll get him stirred up."

The cameraman wasn't convinced and was becoming very upset.

"Look, if we get any closer to that snake he'll head for this boat and there won't be much we can do to stop him," the Reverend explained, keeping the boat at a distance. "So let's leave well enough alone and not ask for trouble."

We finally got the cameraman's feelings soothed somewhat. But to this day he probably thinks we're a couple of cowards. And that's okay with me.

The point I'm trying to make is that John had put it exactly right. And that's just what I tell people when they ask what to do when a snake gets too close for comfort. I tell them the best antidote is a strong dose of preventive medicine: don't get caught in such a fix in the first place. Be smart and let the snake go about his business.

I've heard of more than one fisherman who was killed for being a bit too nosy or playful.

I haven't met a snake yet who had a sense of humor.

I remember one who must have had a good laugh though.

A friend and I were fishing the little Chassahowitzka River in Florida once. We hired a fellow named Jess to handle the boat. He really knew that stream.

Like a lot of rivers in that area, the Chassahowitzka is dotted with big water oak trees. Their branches extend as much as 40 or 50 feet across the water at times, and are so low that a man has to duck down in his boat and work his way through. Before he does, though, it's wise to take an oar and beat the branches, because as often as not there's a snake snoozing up there.

Well, sir, we were making our way along nicely, taking a few bass as we went.

We came to water oak. Jess grabbed the oar and beat the branches before we ducked through. Just as we straightened up—*plop*, a deadly poisonous moccasin dropped from an upper branch right into the boat.

This critter was about three feet long and nobody to fool with, so we all jumped up on the seat.

Jess still had the oar, so I said: "Kill him, Jess!"

"Yes, sir," Jess said. "I'll get him!"

He did all right. Instead of pinning him to the bottom of the boat, he came down too hard with the oar and pushed a board out of the bottom of the old boat. The water was only about three feet deep so we jumped over and pushed the boat to shore. We put the board back but had to keep bailing to stay afloat. Never did know what happened to the snake.

It worked out okay though. We waded ashore, repaired the planking and got underway again. It could have been worse— a lot worse.

But I've had the feeling ever since that there's a big old moccasin snake who's still chuckling to himself somewhere in the Chassahowitzka.

48. *The Reformed Hunter*

IT'S BEEN SAID THERE'S NOTHING WORSE THAN A REFORMED drunk who is always preaching about the evils of drink.

Well, I'm a reformed hunter of sorts. But I'm not one to bend your ear about it. The way I figure it, to each his own. If a man gets a kick out of hunting, fine. I just don't enjoy it much anymore, so I quit.

I'd better go into it a bit to explain, though, because I get a lot of mail asking why I don't hunt.

People can't seem to understand how I can enjoy fishing and not hunting—especially since I once relished it so much. They can't comprehend how I once owned eight bird dogs for ten years, had a small arsenal of firearms and had a car outfitted for hunting—and gave it up clean.

Well, sir, probably the biggest reason I swore off was because there are too many darn fools prowling the woods these days with licenses to kill.

I know. One came within two inches of blowing my brains out. That was cure enough for any man.

It happened one day in the late 1930s up in the Adirondacks. I was picking up a new automobile from a dealer friend in upper New York State, but couldn't get delivery until the next day, so I decided to take advantage of the delay by getting in a little deer hunting in nearby Ausable Forks.

A friend, Tom Gorman, lived just outside town. Tom was a good guy, had a wonderful wife and they had a comfortable place nestled in a fine hunting and fishing area. The food was good too. So I'd stop there when I had a chance on my travels. This time I dropped by and borrowed an automatic rifle before heading for an area that was supposed to have plenty of deer.

I parked my car by the road and walked about a mile into the woods to do a little still hunting. I found a big pine tree and stood by it, hardly moving a muscle and just waiting. Nothing happened and after about three-quarters of an hour I decided to move on.

I had barely moved when all of a sudden a bullet cracked into the pine not two inches above my head followed by an ear-splitting report.

Mister, I hit the ground fast, and I was flatter than a wagon track. I knew immediately what had happened. Some clown had seen my first move, thought I was a deer and shot blindly.

It wasn't blindly though. Rapid fire, a second shot ripped into the tree and a third one—well, I don't know where that one landed. But I sure heard it.

I was never so angry in my life. Scared and boiling mad. At a time like that you feel like you could kill somebody. I mean it.

Well, sir, within seconds this place sounded like the Battle of the Argonne Forest because I started emptying my rifle. I swung toward where the shots had come and fired three times high into the trees. Then I could hear that so-and-so running through the woods.

Boy, that cured me on hunting right there.

Every year you read in the newspapers about the awful number of hunters killed by carelessness in this country. But it's just a statistic. It doesn't penetrate. You tell yourself it always happens to the other fellow. It couldn't happen to you.

Well, I came within an eyelash of being the "other fellow!" I was nearly a statistic. You have to be nearly killed by some bloody fool to get the full impact.

I was lucky once. I might not be so fortunate next time. So there won't be any next time for me.

I've rarely picked up a rifle in the more than 25 years since.

I did go for some quail last year near Lake Charles, Louisiana. But that was more for novelty than anything else. And that's odd to say because at one time I used to hunt almost as much as I fished—especially quail, duck, bear and some wild hog.

But I never really went for deer hunting. I would never give a nickel for it.

There are a couple of explanations, I suppose.

For some reason, I never cottoned to killing a deer. There's something about them. It's odd, because I never had any qualms about killing a bear. It's just something I can't fully explain. Maybe it's a deer's tranquillity. I know part of it is that so many deer bagged every year are little more than fawns. I've seen deer lugged out of woods no bigger than collie dogs.

An incident I remember well really soured me. Coincidentally, it happened up in the Adirondacks, not too far from where I was almost shot a few years later.

On this particular trip a friend said: "Gad, all the neighbors are going deer hunting. Come along."

Now these people were mostly farmers and, as I found out, their idea of a hunt is to spread across on a line and drive the deer out ahead of them. They put me in a spot where they'd drive through, in a valley between two big hills where the deer would have to travel through a gap no wider than 75 or 80 feet.

So I grabbed my movie camera and rifle and went ahead.

Well, sir, it wasn't long before I heard the men coming, thirteen of them spread out and making all sorts of noises, barking like dogs and whatnot. And right in front of them came about a dozen doe, and not a buck among them.

They were a beautiful sight, some of them no farther than 15 or 20 feet from my hiding place as they narrowed through the gap. It was really something.

I started shooting—my camera, not my gun.

When the drovers came through they were all excited.

"How many did you get?" they asked.

"Heck," I said, "they were only doe."

I guess they were pretty disgusted with me.

But let me tell you something. I'm not going to slaughter any doe. I'd have shot a 10-point buck maybe, but no doe.

The whole thing sort of turned my stomach. What kind of sport is that? I never went "hunting" with those boys again.

Butchering fawn is one reason for my dislike of deer hunting. Another is something I mentioned before—the careless hunter. These maniacs seem to gravitate to deer hunting like pieces of iron to a magnet.

Let me tell you about another near catastrophe that underscores what I'm talking about.

This happened in upper New York State too—near Saranac

153

Lake—just about the time I nearly got hit. I was friendly with a manager of a sporting goods store there named Cheeseman. I used to sell him tackle, and the first thing he'd always say was, "Gad, let's go hunting." And over a span of six years or so we invariably did.

One time he said: "Gad, I've got a man with me from Washington, D.C. He's a nice gentleman and a well-educated person. He wants to go deer hunting with us."

The three of us drove about five miles out of town and parked along the road.

"Gad, walk up that hill and you'll come to a burned-out shack. Wait there."

He told his friend to take another route, following a brook across a beaver dam.

Then he said: "I'll go farther down and cross over the ridge. Stay on the ridges and I'll drive toward you."

The idea, of course, was to drive any deer in the area into a shrinking triangle as we made our rendezvous.

Well, sir, I reached the burned shack first and flopped down with my back against a tree. In no time at all the man from Washington arrived over the dam and sat down on my left.

We waited about twenty minutes before it happened. And I'll never forget it.

This fellow suddenly froze and got a wild look in his eyes.

"I hear a deer," he whispered in a frantic sort of way.

I didn't say a word, just motioned for him to be quiet. Then he reached over and grabbed my arm. This boy was really getting excited. He grabbed the rifle from his lap, the left hand on the barrel, the right hand on the stock.

"There's a deer in there!" he said in that frantic whisper.

This time I grabbed his gun.

"Damn it, be quiet!" I hollered, purposely loud enough to scare anything away. "That's Cheeseman coming through there!"

And just about that moment old Cheeseman came strolling through the opening where this guy had been wanting to shoot. And let me tell you this other fellow just wilted.

"My God!" he said. "I could have killed him!"

"Never tell him what I almost did. I'll never go in the woods again as long as I live."

See what happens to some so-called hunters? They lose their heads. This man never thought of Cheeseman when he heard the noise. All he could think of was a deer. It bordered on temporary insanity.

It scares the wits out of a man.

Now I'm not condemning all deer hunters. Only a small percentage are trigger happy. But that's too many.

It takes *only one* to make you a statistic!

49. The One That Got Away

IT WAS SO QUIET THE STILLNESS WAS DEAFENING.

I mean you could hear a mosquito scratch his nose at fifty paces.

All of a sudden the whole Chassahowitzka River exploded around me.

I had been casting for bass with a top water plug. What I got instead was a tarpon well over six feet and 100 pounds.

Brother, talk about having a tiger by the tail!

I've hooked a lot of game tarpon in my days. But this one was the livest wire of them all—especially tough to handle because I hadn't been expecting him.

The little Chassahowitzka had some mighty fine bass fishing in those days, and in the fall some of the finest sea trout in all of Florida. It's located about 50 miles north of Tampa and is only about six miles long, flowing out of a spring into the Gulf of Mexico.

I had been drifting down with a wonderful fishing partner named Boyd Jay when we came to a spot where a big tree had been uprooted.

"There's got to be one king-sized hole under there," I said to Boyd. "Watch me pick a big bass out of it."

I cast a plug just where I wanted it and let it set a second before popping it two, three, four times.

That's when that big baby hit and turned my world upside down.

I mean that monster really hit. He went into the air at least 10 feet and did a somersault before diving again. When he came up a second time he catapulted like one of those underwater sea-to-air missiles you see in the newsreels—and no more than 10 feet ahead of our boat.

This time that tarpon did the niftiest one-and-a-half gainer you'd ever want to see before belly-flopping—right into our laps!

Boy, we left that boat in a hurry, and I don't mean maybe.

Those tarpon are powerful creatures and can break a man's arm or leg like a match stick, pounding around a boat like a trip hammer. And this one proved it. He knocked Boyd's tackle box overboard, upset mine all over the boat and snapped a rod before finally flipping over the side himself.

Mister, that's the kind of fish a man remembers. That incident must have happened twenty-five years ago, but I recall every terrifying second of it.

That's why I'm mentioning it here. I get a lot of letters from people asking about the fish I remember best.

Well, sir, I've caught record fish and I've caught prize fish. But outside of that first tiny catfish I caught on the little Okaw River as a boy, this tarpon has to be it.

Thank heaven he got away!

50. Bears, Bulls and Boars

THE NAME OF THE GAME IS FISHING. BUT SOMETIMES IT involves more game than fish.

A man goes out hunting for fish. But he ends up coming across a lot of other critters along the way. And, in a wink, they change him from the hunter to the hunted.

I've been chased by some pretty mean animals over the years: bears, bulls, boars—you name it.

They can be pretty frantic beasts, and all I had to defend myself with was a fishing rod. And, mister, that isn't much help. What's a man going to do with it—flog the poor devil to death?

I'll give you a few examples of what I mean.

A friend named Herb Lant and I were fishing for bass one day after World War II just below Clewiston, Florida. That's on the southwest edge of Lake Okeechobee and on the northern fringe of the Everglades. It's flat, treeless country—a sort of prairie dotted here and there by grazing cattle.

The area we were fishing was grooved with drainage canals —all thick with bigmouth bass.

Marshes rim those canals so that you can only drive an automobile within a couple of hundred yards or so of the water, and walk the rest of the way.

Well, sir, we had been fishing one canal for an hour or so and had taken some pretty good bass—up to 8-pounders. We were just playing around, catching them and turning them loose.

It was getting toward supper hour. Herb figured it was time to be getting back.

"Just give me a few more minutes, Herb," I said. "There's a couple of 10- and 12-pound beauties in here and I'd like to get one."

"Go ahead," he said. "I'll wait at the car. There's something I want to look at under the hood anyway. The carburetor's been acting a little strange."

Herb was always tinkering with cars. It was his business. He owned a fine gas station in Schenectady where I traded. He knew what an automobile was all about.

He hadn't been gone but a couple of minutes when I heard him hollering and honking the car horn like to wake up the dead. I couldn't make out what he was yelling, but I could see by his wild gestures that he wanted me to turn around.

I finally did—and almost dropped where I stood.

A big brown steer was bearing down on me. I mean this old boy was as big as a house and had fire in his eyes. He had his head down and was on the dead run, making tracks straight for me.

Well, sir, I should have known better than to have been in a fix like this in the first place. I had known right well that some of these cattle could be mean. But the whole time I'd been fishing I hadn't given them a thought. It was just pure and simple carelessness.

It was too late to bawl myself out though. I was the target of a one-steer stampede and had no place to hide. There wasn't a hole or a tree in sight. About the only thing to climb was a blade of grass.

I'll tell you something, mister: my old heart was pounding to beat the band.

It's funny how a man's mind reacts to an emergency. An old story I'd once read about a cowboy in a similar situation flashed through my head. He had side-stepped the animal at the last instant. So I decided to try the same thing. That's about all I could do.

So I set my feet, ready to spring aside.

Meanwhile, Herb was honking the horn, hollering and jumping up and down trying to distract the beast.

It didn't do any good. That animal had me zeroed in and just kept coming. I can't say exactly how fast he was traveling because he wasn't wearing a speedometer. But it was as quick as four hoofs will carry one of those creatures.

Well, sir, he got within 10 feet of me and did something I still can't figure to this day. He didn't break speed but suddenly veered off to my left. Instead of me side-stepping him, he had side-stepped me.

The steer plowed past me—so close the suction darn near knocked me over—clear into the canal. There was an awful splash when he hit the water. Then he calmly waded up to his belly, walked out the other side and began eating grass.

I thought I'd die. I don't know what this steer had had in mind. But he sure had scared me half to death. If my heart didn't quit that day it never will.

It had been tested pretty good years before—and the culprit may have been that steer's father.

A fellow named Jim Baker and I had taken some bass on a stream outside of Mt. Pleasant, Iowa. On the way back to the car we cut through a farm. I was about two-thirds of the way across an open field and Jim was about 40 feet ahead of me. When he reached the barbed-wire fence, he stooped to get through. As he did, he twisted around toward me—turning ghost white as he did.

"Look out!" Jim yelled.

I turned just in time to see a big old red bull bearing down on me. He had a head of steam up and was traveling like nothing they ever saw in those arenas of Old Mexico.

I still had on hip boots and couldn't move fast, but managed to reach the fence. I hit the ground and rolled underneath an instant before that doggone bull arrived. I mean I could feel the heat of his breath.

One second slower and I wouldn't have done much more gaddin' about.

So I've had my fill of cattle.

I've had better luck with the bears.

Back in 1939 at Bingham, Maine, I had a little experience with a momma bear and her two cubs that I'll never forget.

Austin Stream up there is a dandy. It's nestled in a beautiful setting and features plenty of nice brook trout.

You have to drive over a little bridge off the main road and park in about a mile before climbing a good-sized hill. When you hit the top, there's the stream below, set in a valley between two hills rising at a 45-degree angle.

Well, sir, I went there set to catch me a mess of trout. And right quick I hooked four or five 13-inch brookies.

All of a sudden I looked up and saw the old sow and her cubs. The cubs were frolicking on the opposite hill and the bear was in the stream up a way. Just when I saw them, the bear raised up on her haunches and began sniffing. For some reason she didn't see me. But she sure sensed something.

I froze. Fortunately the little breeze there was was coming to me, not away from me where she could get my scent.

Still, two things really disturbed me.

One was the cubs. If the bear had been alone I would have let her see me. She would have turned tail and taken off, as scared of me as I was of her. But with cubs to protect it was different. She'd challenge and fight.

The other was that I was cut off. If the bear charged me, I couldn't get away. I could never make it over the hill. It was much too steep.

She sniffed some more, then dropped down and inched a bit closer. She still didn't see me. But she knew things weren't right. Finally she let out an awful grunt and those frisky cubs took off over the hill. Old momma stayed though. She stayed a long time, sniffing, and from time to time edging more in my direction.

Now she was within 60 feet of me, but for some reason still couldn't see me. The only difference between me and a statue at that point was that I was perspiring plenty. Finally that bear just splashed out of the stream and lumbered up after her cubs.

When she got over the hill, this old man took off over the opposite one.

I had an even stranger experience with another bear in Bingham the year before.

Harold Collins was Bingham postmaster then. He and I decided to go up to Carry Pond for brook trout one day in mid-May.

We cut off Route 201, the old Benedict Arnold Trail to Canada, crossed a bridge over the Kennebec and went about three miles up a side road before parking. Then we started to walk another three miles up a small mountain to the pond.

About a mile in, Harold stopped and turned around.

"Look who's following us," he said.

Well, sir, there was a half-grown bear back about 100 yards.

To make a long story short, every time we moved, he moved. And every time we stopped, he stopped. It was like a comedy. Almost. We were unarmed, with just a fly rod apiece. We weren't overly frightened. We had a good lead on the bear, and if he started to make a run at us we'd have had a little time to make a move. There were plenty of trees handy, and he would be running on wet ground.

But what concerned us was the bear's strange behavior— mimicking our every move. I had never heard of such a thing. And neither had Harold, who was born and raised in that country.

Finally I said, "Let's walk—fast. Maybe we can outwalk him."

Well, sir, this bear walked too—and fast. For a mile he kept up with us—step for step—but keeping his distance. Meanwhile, our legs were going like pistons and our necks were getting stiff from looking behind us as we went.

Finally, about a mile from the pond, the bear turned off and wandered into the timber—disappearing as easily as he had appeared.

So Harold and I got out of that one easy.

I wasn't so lucky with another animal, one day before World War II, in Yankeetown, Florida, about 70 miles north of Tampa.

Bud Kelley and I were fishing the Withlacoochee River and staying at a camp about 100 yards in from shore.

One twilight, darkness was setting in fast. I docked the boat and said to Bud, "You go on ahead. Get the lamp lit and the skillet on the stove. I'll take care of the gear and be up in a minute."

I stowed the boat and tackle and headed up the road toward the camp. It was just a little narrow path, really, flanked by swamps about 200 feet of the way up.

As I said, it was getting dark quick. But a little way up I thought I saw something move in the path ahead. I stopped, squinted—and my eyes darn near popped clean out of their sockets.

Standing not 20 feet dead ahead was a wild boar and his girl friend. And, brother, was he ever mean and ugly! And he must have weighed 300 pounds. I mean it.

Well, sir, he started snorting and grunting, and I suspected this was no time or place to argue about right of way or anything else.

A second later I was convinced of it.

That old red boy started for me and I left that road like a grey squirrel. My first step off the path was in the mud; I left both my moccasins there and made one mighty leap for the nearest tree.

It turned out to be a little tree. But at least it was something to climb. Still, I didn't feel any too safe standing on a limb no bigger in circumference than my thumb. And only a few feet below that boar and his sow fussed and fretted. He did not want me around. He wouldn't budge without her, and she wasn't about to leave.

Well, sir, I figured I had two chances.

One was Bud. I told myself he'd miss me and come looking. Secretly, I knew better. It was a good bet he had put his head on a pillow for a minute. And once that boy shuts his eyes, forget it. He's gone—dead to the world. You're not going to wake him up with an atom bomb.

The other hope was a fellow named Old Man Smith. He was a deer hunter, and his place wasn't but 200 yards away. In fact I could see a light coming from his house through the trees.

I started hollering. Smith had about seventy-five hounds. I figured my yelling might get them agitated. It did. They all began barking up a storm.

My plan paid off—eventually.

When the dogs started yapping I could hear the old man open his front door and cuss at them to be quiet. I hollered to him, but he couldn't hear me above the racket. He went back inside and slammed the door.

I nearly died.

An hour later I was still in the tree and the hounds were still sounding off. Finally Smith knew there had to be something serious to keep them stirred up so long. He came out searching to see what the trouble was, and the dogs led him straight to me.

The hounds shooed off the wild hogs and I climbed down.

I'll never forget old Smith standing there, hands on hips, and giving me the business.

"What's the matter with you, Gad?" he said. "You ought to be ashamed, trying to separate a boy from his lady friend! Ain't you got no romance in your soul?"

Romance wasn't exactly what I had in my mind for Kelley at that moment either. I stormed up the trail and into the shack.

And there he was: sprawled out on his cot sawing wood.

Yes, sir, old Bud is really something.

And so are some of the strange critters a fisherman runs into between streams.

51.   *The Frustration of Fishing*

FISH ARE STRANGE CREATURES.

They're even more unpredictable than women—and that's going some.

How can you figure fish?

One day a man can be sitting on top of a school so thick that those devils seem to be in platoon formation. He'll drop some appetizing bait in among them and get nothing. I mean he couldn't stir those critters with a rifle.

Another day a man will catch his popping bug on a reed a foot above the surface and a bass will explode out of nowhere and pluck it off.

You explain it to me.

Just don't try to tell me that you can read a fish's thoughts and know why he acts like he does. That's one thing in this world I absolutely won't buy. There is no such thing as a mind reader of fish.

If I ever had any doubts, they were cleared up pronto during a trip to Washington, D.C., years ago. I was visiting a friend who was an official with the Fish and Wildlife Service in the Department of the Interior. We got to talking about what makes fish tick.

"Forget it, Gad," he said. "See those cabinets lining that

wall? And see that green door over there? It leads to another room filled with more files. They're all crammed with research done on the matter and with a million and one ideas from people who think they know. The verdict: nobody—and I mean *nobody*—knows what fish are *really* thinking."

Now don't get me wrong. I'm not saying that fishing is strictly pot luck and that good and bad fishermen alike have an equal chance. That's not it at all. Fishing is a gamble, and the better a man knows his business and the habits of his prey the more he's going to cut down the odds.

What I mean is that even the most expert of anglers, using every technique in the book, will come up with dry days. He can slice the percentages; but no matter how much he knows he'll never have a sure thing, because it still all boils down to the mood of the fish—something nobody can explain.

As I've written earlier, as a teen-ager I'd lie on a log on the lip of a slew along the Ohio River studying the habits of bass by the hour. I'd watch his reactions and how those responses would vary. A friend would cast the same plug into the bed of the very same bass on two consecutive days and get two totally different reactions. One day that fish would face the plug, gently nose up to it, examine it and leave it alone. The next day the same bass would be on top of the same plug like lightning.

A matter of hunger? Maybe, but I doubt it. To my way of thinking, a plug doesn't look like anything good to eat. I just think a bass is a pugnacious savage who likes to kill—when he's in the mood.

The same contrariness is pretty much true of all fish—smart ones like the brown trout, and dumb ones such as the eastern brook trout.

I'm amused when I hear a fisherman make a cast and say, "Gee, that trout missed my fly!"

Don't kid yourself, brother. He didn't miss it. No fish does. He just didn't want it. If he did, you couldn't keep it away from him.

Hundreds of times I've had a fish strike at my bait four or five times. He wasn't missing it. He didn't want it. He was merely toying with it. But, boy, if he wants it, look out. Even in muddy water where he mightn't be able to see a plug too well, he'll hear it and kill it.

One of the biggest strings of bass I ever took was at Greer's Ferry in Arkansas not too long ago. Now that's a murky lake after the spring run-off. But I put a top water plug out there, danced it around a bit, and got all the fish I could handle. A lot of people won't fish water like that. But don't pass it up. Try surface lures and you may be in for the surprise of your life. If there are bass in there, they'll hear it or see it and may strike.

That's if they're in the mood, of course—the name of the game. If they aren't, forget it.

I'll never forget an incident on Cape Cod years ago that's as good an example as any of what I'm talking about.

All the Boston and New Bedford papers were full of stories of how there were no stripers running on the Cape. Nobody was catching any. In those days if people didn't see birds working over a school, they didn't figure there were any fish around.

One day a Boston sports writer telephoned me.

"What's happened to the stripers, Gad?" he asked.

"They're out there," I said. "But they're not moving."

"That's hard to believe," he said.

"Join the club," I said. "Nobody believes it."

"How do you know they're out there?" he asked.

"I've seen them—big schools of them," I said. "Come on down and I'll show you."

He did and I did.

We boated over to a long stretch of beach and drifted to a spot offshore where the water was only about six feet deep.

"Oh my gosh!" the writer swooned. "I see it, but I don't believe it!"

There they were—a school that would average from 5- to 20-pound stripers in a line that stretched fully a mile and a half.

I took a spoon and touched one. He just moved over. I took a big sea worm and actually dragged it across the nose of another and he wasn't interested. Those bass wouldn't touch anything.

"I'm afraid to write this," the writer said. "Nobody will believe me—just like nobody believes you."

"Well, you'd better write it," I said. "Someday very soon these beauties are going to start moving. And when they do, all heaven is going to break loose around here."

And it did about four days later, to provide some fabulous, fabulous fishing that ran for weeks.

Why did those stripers lie dead one day and move the next?

I can't tell you. Nobody can. People have all sorts of theories on what makes a fish tick, and they're welcome to them. Me, I don't have a theory. There is no answer to the riddle of what makes a fish so unpredictable. I've seen too many contradictions.

Take a little thing like wading a stream.

Naturally the worst thing a fisherman can do is burst across —*bang, bang, bang*—like an old cow plowing across a pasture. Most times you'll spook a fish 50 feet away doing something like that. Heck, you can scare a fish a good distance off sometimes even when you're careful. Yet in the very same stream I've seen a clumsy wader go charging across and come so close to a fish that he could have shaken hands with him.

So who knows?

Or take a river where the fish are biting good in the morning. An angler climbs out for a little lunch. When he returns he can't get a strike to save his life. He changes flies. Still nothing. Let's even say there's a hatch on this river all of a sudden and the fish begin rising all around. The man matches up the fly with the hatch pretty well—say using a No. 10. Nothing. Okay, just for the heck of it, he changes to a No. 16. *Bing-o*—he's got himself a fish.

Frustrating? Yes-sir-ee, boy. I guess it's all part of the cat-and-mouse game between fish and fisherman that makes the sport so intriguing. I mean if you got a fish every time you baited a hook, it would get a little boring and you'd soon lose interest.

That happens from time to time, of course. I was on the Rupert River in northern Quebec once when every time I threw a fly out I got a squaretail. And I mean right quick every time, mister. Now that isn't fishing. It's just plain monotony, but it's fun.

That doesn't happen very often, and I'm happy it doesn't.

What fun would fishing be if a man didn't have to work for every catch?

Friend, that's the fun of fishing!

52. The Angry Angler

Four things in this fishing game really get my dander up and turn me into the angry angler.

They are water pollution, the squandering of fish, erratic stocking and phony fish stories.

There are others, but these top my list.

Ordinarily I'm an easy-going, peaceful man. Not much bothers me so long as I have someplace to lay my head and something to put in my belly. And, thank the Lord, I've never been without either.

But these four pet peeves really upset and ignite me, exciting me like a worm on a hot rock.

I can try to do something about the needless, wasteful pollution. And I am, because I'm convinced it is one of our country's most serious internal problems today and will be one of its biggest national headaches in ten years if something isn't done about it quickly. So I've made a personal cause—a real crusade—out of helping to alert people on pollution.

I can also do a little something on the wasting of fish and inconsistent overstocking policies by focusing attention on them too.

What I can't do much about is fish fiction. You can't stop a man from writing phony fish stories he passes off as the Bible truth, as long as editors keep printing them. Besides, I guess this problem is more irritating than serious anyway.

These lies would be almost amusing except there are so many and they fool so many people.

I'd estimate the majority of the fishing stories that appear in the national men's and sporting magazines are built up; many of them exaggerated something fierce. And some are outright fakes. It's a disgrace.

Let's get the record straight. There are some mighty fine outdoor writers, and they come up with some excellent features. I have no quarrel with these stories and I enjoy them.

I'm talking about the others—so many, many others. Talk about *fish* stories!

I hate misrepresentation, and this is what so many of these stories are.

Why don't they just say it's fiction? I enjoy a good fishing yarn. But don't try to kid me, brother. Don't say it's the truth and then lie.

I don't go along with such fabrication. I really don't. It rubs against my grain.

Look. You and I can go out tomorrow into any body of water in the world. We can pick up some fish somewhere and make an awful good story about how we caught them there. But the truth is there's not a darn thing to it.

The part that really galls me is the deceit involved.

I mean how can the average reader know what's truth and what isn't? Unless he's been to these places, he doesn't. He takes the writer's word. And too many writers take advantage of that trust.

Although I know better than to believe him, this type of writer has taken something away from me too. Because I know so many stories are fake, I pretty much leave these "true" stories alone now. I just don't have the inclination to read them anymore.

And this hurts, because I used to be an avid reader.

As I've said, I'm a confirmed night owl. After normal people went to bed I used to love to sit and read till two or three o'clock in the morning. I'd devour any reading material I could get my hands on—especially history and mystery books, and the popular men's and outdoor magazines.

Well, sir, these phony fishing writers have cheated me because I will not read these articles very often anymore. So I miss out on the ones that are really honest.

So, you bet I'm angry.

I'm plenty sore about all the squandered fish I see too.

Boy, I get furious when I head in toward a lake or river and see dead fish or their bones scattered along the side of the road or the shore. Hard to believe? You bet it is. Yet I see it all the time. And it's all because of unthinking, selfish so-and-sos who ought to know better.

I think it's terrific when a man can take his limit—and use them. But don't let me catch him throwing them away to rot afterward. A man should know before he starts how many fish he can use. After he catches what he needs, sure keep on fishing—but throw the extras back as fast as they're taken.

You'd be surprised by the number of letters I get from

people who see me turn a fish loose on television. They can't understand why I do it. I can't use him, that's why. Unless I want a fish for supper, or somebody else does, I'll throw that fish back every time. Why should I keep the fish and let him waste when I can put him back and let somebody else have the enjoyment of catching him that I had?

It's just common sense.

Proper stocking is also a matter of common sense, but some states don't exercise it. Now a lot of states are way ahead in this business of stocking fish. But it's the ones who are behind that bewilder and bother me.

Some are neglectful and make no effort to stock enough fish. Others overstock, which is almost as bad. I mean fish in a lake are like cattle on a range. Both need so much food per measurement of area. Like a steer, if a fish doesn't get enough eatables he'll either die off or his growth will be stunted.

I guess there are a lot of reasons for improper stocking. Some of it is ignorance. Some of it is because somebody big in the State House doesn't care. And some of it is because somebody big in the State House cares too much. I've seen lakes that are continually overstocked because certain individuals fish there. Thank heaven this favoritism isn't too common, but it happens more often than it should.

Whatever the reason, the results are the same: fishermen are cheated—and at least one gets plenty hot under the collar.

Now about water pollution and its relation to fish.

Let me give you fair warning before I start. I've just been warming up so far. If you don't want to hear an old man climbing a soap box and sounding off, stop right here and skip on to the next chapter, brother. Or if you don't want to risk being offended, you'd better quit here too, because I'm going to do some serious ear-bending and step on a few toes for the next few pages.

I have a quarrel and I've got to get it off my chest.

I can't emphasize the danger of water pollution enough, and never miss an opportunity to say so when I'm talking to local newspaper, radio and television boys or when I'm on coast-to-coast promotion tours. I tell politicians about it too.

We've got to move and move fast to slow this problem down or our country will be in serious, serious trouble in ten years. I mean there won't be a body of water left fit for man or beast in the good old U.S.A. Pretty soon there won't be any drinking water, any fish. And there won't be a decent place to swim.

Don't just shrug and pass it off, mister. You're the one who is going to suffer. And you can do something about it.

Now I'm not an engineer or biologist or polished writer. So I can't explain the problem in fancy words and technical terms. I wish I could. All I can do is try to tell it the best way I can—with one-syllable words, very simple facts and plain talk. I've seen the situation develop first-hand over the last fifty years.

First, what is pollution?

I looked it up in the dictionary once. Webster defines the word pollute as "to make or render unclean; to defile; desecrate; profane." Mr. Webster knows his words, although I could add a few perhaps less printable meanings.

What it comes down to is that our whole way of living is being endangered and people at all levels are guilty: towns, industry and just plain citizens. A town drains its sewage into a river rather than build a sewage plant. A factory dumps its old oil, a mill its sawdust, pulp scraps, or other industrial waste, into a river, rather than dispose of it another way. An individual will litter a river with trash rather than throw it on a dump. The reasons vary. But whoever the offender and whatever his reason, the result is the same: water pollution.

What happens basically is this:

Waste is dumped into a body of water and settles on rocks, either on the bottom or along the shore. The refuse may be so poisonous that it kills every living thing in the water almost immediately. Or it may take a little longer. The scum that forms chokes the algae and smothers the insect life that fish feed on. Without food, fish die.

So one way or another, you're killing the fish. The contamination of drinking and swimming water is obvious. If the water is too dirty for fish it's got to be too dirty for human beings.

Like I've said, I've been watching the situation going to Hades for fifty years.

I remember when I first began fishing and traveling. I saw many streams where you could reach down, scoop your hat and come up with clear, pure drinking water. You'd better not try that today. More often than not you'd get a bellyache that wouldn't quit, and it might just kill you.

You didn't hear much about pollution back then. That was before the big industrial booms and population explosion and

169

before most of the industries and people were aware of the problem.

I can recall back before World War I fishing a river in the Middle West. That was a fine river then. You could catch bass just about anywhere. Today that river is nothing but a running sewer.

I mention this river, but it's only one of thousands upon thousands of contaminated bodies of water from coast to coast. All across this country most of our streams are polluted. The only general exceptions are in the Far West, and even some of these are falling by the wayside too. It's a shame.

Put your finger almost anywhere on the map and it's pretty much the same story.

There's another river in the Midwest that's a good example. It once was a good river—before a plant was built along it that began dumping all its waste into the river, killing every fish for miles. Every year the town fines the company $25. I suppose the company is a big taxpayer to this little community and employs a lot of people there, so the town doesn't want to risk losing it. It merely slaps it on the wrist. Imagine, a $25 fine! Naturally the company gladly writes out a check (heck, it could take it out of petty cash) and keeps on merrily dumping—and killing.

The Ausable River in upper New York has always been a beautiful fishing stream, as far down as Ausable Forks, where the east and west branches meet. The state is doing an excellent job of keeping this section of the river well stocked. However, from this point on, this river was for many years heavily polluted by sewage. Now a sewage disposal plant is being installed and plans made to reclaim this part of the river below the Forks.

I'll never forget flying over the shore of Lake Erie once when the water was low. The bottom looked like a junk yard. It was shocking.

Remember when blue pike dinners were a big thing? No more. Fleets of commercial fishermen used to comb Lake Erie and come out with plenty of blue pike. They were fabulous fish for food. Between pollution and the U.S. and Canadian governments netting them as commercial fish, a fisherman can hardly find them anymore. Just recently there's been a government movement to bring these fish back. But I'll tell you something, mister: it'll be a lot tougher bringing them back than it was getting rid of them.

There was a report I read a year or so ago that explained how pollution circulated in Lake Michigan. And it should open a few eyes. Somebody did a study and found that a circular current runs continuously counter-clockwise from the Chicago area to a point about 100 miles out. So all that polluted water never goes anywhere but out and back, around and around.

Tampa used to have a big problem, but the city cleared it up during World War II.

The city would dump all its sewage into the Hillsboro River, which runs right through Tampa. Over the years all this refuse built up and became a menace. When the temperature was right and there wasn't any wind, you could smell the odor for miles. It made the Chicago stock yards smell like a perfume factory by comparison. It was said that it even caused the paint to peel off many houses along Tampa Bay.

The only good thing about it was that it made for excellent tarpon fishing. Tarpon love dirty water, so they had a picnic there. So did the fishermen, enjoying some of the world's greatest tarpon fishing. Boy, that water was filthy. You could take up anchor 30 miles out into the bay and pull up a rock coated with scum.

Finally, about twenty-five years ago, the town put in a big sanitation plant and cleaned up that mess. The tarpon left the river in town, but who cared? It was great for the city. And it wasn't bad for fishermen either. The tarpon soon disappeared, but the tides soon brought in plenty of other fish—sea trout, redfish, mullet and snook.

I've stayed clear of mentioning Maine so far in this pollution business because I wanted to save it for last.

Now I love that state, I really do. It's beautiful in so many ways. But sometimes you're extra hard on the ones you love. I suppose it's because you do love them and care enough to want to make them even better. So I have to be hard on Maine because it's guilty, like many other states, of failing to take enough anti-pollution measures.

Take the Bangor Pool on the Penobscot River. Salmon from the Atlantic Ocean used to run up there every spring. It was a big thing and was publicized nationally. The first salmon caught was always presented to the President of the United States.

I used to fish it plenty 30 years ago. It was beautiful fishing. Now, I haven't heard of salmon being caught there in six years. The Penobscot is more than a little polluted from Bangor on down. The people know about this but it will take some time to reclaim this part of the river after the plans for pollution control are put into effect.

The Kennebec River, where I've fished for 35 years, is feeling pollution, too. The paper mills and other industries have used the river for their wastes and the lower end is now getting the "end" results of this pollution. There is a power company that contributes its share toward keeping this river from being as productive as it should be for a good fish population. At this time cities, towns, and industries on the Penobscot and Kennebec and other rivers are making studies and other definite plans for water-pollution control.

I have watched at times during the summer (and winter, too)—take a Sunday, when there isn't much pull on the power—when those people will cut the flow to almost nothing. The rocks become exposed to the bright sunlight, and dry air, so the food for fish is killed off. Couldn't the state pass a law which would control the water flow, not a power company?

I've seen it work in other places successfully. Take Bureau of Reclamation's dam out in Jackson Hole country on the Snake River in Wyoming.

I filmed a float trip out there recently. The boys who make their living along it were telling me how the federal government people control it wonderfully. They never let it get too high or too low. After the big spring runoff, when the water gets normal, the government regulates an even flow at all times. And around September, when the dry fly fishing is at its best, they regulate the water even lower so that the average man can wade and fish.

This is what's happening more and more—especially in the areas of those reclamation dams. That's what could be done in the East. That area doesn't have the dams yet, to regulate water as it should, but it's going to have to get around to it. It will have to in order to get more power and control that awful pollution that's spoiling what could be some of the world's finest fishing.

And so it goes—pollution from coast to coast. I've mentioned only a tiny fraction of the list. But it's senseless to mention any more. The heart of the matter is what can be done about it.

I know it's easy to sit back and criticize, difficult to make concrete, constructive suggestions. Like I've said before, I don't know all the answers. But I have a few ideas that can help.

It's up to every state in the Union as well as the federal government to put teeth into their anti-pollution laws and then enforce them. All offenders must be cracked down on—hard.

And since it's up to government, it's up to you. Everyone can help. You can because we live in a democracy where the government represents the wishes of the people. I know a lot of people have become skeptical of that. You know, that old saw about "you can't beat city hall" and such.

Mister, don't fool yourself. Don't ever feel you're helpless just because you're only one little voice. If you do you're licked from the start. You can do plenty.

I'll give you a case in point.

I was on a trip in Maine not so long ago in an area I often fish. I pulled into a little gas station. A boy there told me the river nearby was filled with oil. I checked into it right away, even before I unpacked my gear. The boy was right.

I traced the trouble up the river to a mill. I saw that oil floating downstream, settling on everything it touched: shore line, rocks, branches, bushes, insect life and eventually fish.

You can imagine how long it took me to collar the State Water Improvement Commission. They launched an immediate investigation.

Now my point is simple. I may be wrong, but I think I got action because I was R. V. Gaddis The Citizen, not Gadabout Gaddis The Flying Fisherman. I'm convinced you'd get the same action too.

So let your representatives know how strongly you feel about pollution. They're not mind readers. You elected them and they're your agents.

After all, you've got a squawk coming. You're losing drinking and swimming water. You're losing fish. And who do you think is going to get stuck with the tab for cleaning up this mess?

It's you, Mr. Taxpayer. You're it.

And don't kid yourself about this pollution business: it's an expensive, expensive proposition.

The federal government has a program going on it. So do some states. Some manufacturers too. But it's going to cost billions.

I believe New York State alone last year appropriated a

173

fantastic sum to curb pollution on the Hudson River. Now you talk about a polluted stream! That Hudson is a pip.

A lot of people believe a stream can be cleaned up overnight. They think it's a simple matter that can be done anytime. Well let me put them straight: it takes a lot of time as well as a lot of money.

And, as I've said, you're the one who's going to get stuck with the bill.

The frightening part is that this whole problem is going to get a lot worse before it gets better. One reason is that the mess will get more messy every day that goes by without anything being done. Another is that it will multiply because of the exploding population. It's a vicious circle. The more people, the more refuse there'll be, the more factories there'll be, the more fishermen there'll be. Yet the more people, the more drinking and swimming water will be needed and the more fish will be needed.

Water is getting more precious by the day. Water levels aren't up to par, and they probably never will be again because of the ever-increasing population. But there will be enough water—plenty—if it's cleaned up, saved and protected. We won't have enough if it continues to be abused and wasted. It's as simple as that.

I could go on and on, but I'm sure you get what I'm trying to say. I just want to help alert people about pollution's tremendous dangers. I hope you'll do yourself a favor and do something about it. I hope you'll read more about it, because one of these days it's going to come to a vote in some shape or form, and a man ought to know what he's voting for. So talk about it and keep on your representatives about it. And when you see some wrong-doing, do something about it—immediately.

These are the only ways we'll get rid of this problem and avoid a national catastrophe. And the sooner we do the better.

Like I've said, it's coming out of your pocket as well as mine.

And if you won't do it for yourself, do it for your kids' sake. They're the ones who'll be paying for our sins in years to come.

53. *See America First*

LYNDON JOHNSON SAID IT FIRST.

When the President advised us citizens to "See America First," he said a mouthful—even for a Texan. He put into three short words something I've felt for a long, long time.

A man can spend a lifetime traveling around this big, wonderful land of ours and still not see it all.

I know—believe me, do I *ever* know!

I'm going to get a little big-headed here and say there are few men alive who have seen this country as I have. It's taken no particular talent—just a lot of years of doing, that's all.

Yet I've only seen a fraction of America The Beautiful.

This is the reason I've never had the yearning to globetrot. People know my gypsy appetite and can't understand why I haven't traveled around the world—or at least to Europe. Sure I'd like to see it all someday—after I've seen all of America. I've got to get over a love affair with this country first.

Want to know what amuses me? It's these people who drive from coast to coast and then insist they've seen the country.

"Fine," I say. "How long did it take you?"

"Five days," they answer.

Can you beat that?

I'll tell you exactly what they saw: nothing!

Mister, if you can see these United States in five days from the window of an automobile going 70 miles per hour over a super highway, you're a better man than I. Man, this land is just too darn big and there's too much to see.

Yet people argue with me.

"Okay, Gad," they say. "So you don't see every square inch of land and every cubic foot of water. What's the difference? If you get an idea of what every region is like, that's enough. The rest is just repetition."

I can't agree with that—not a bit.

I've fished thousands of streams and lakes in this country and have never found two alike. Similar maybe, but not the same. Each has something distinctive, a charm of its very own. And I can say the same thing about the land too.

I can give example after example of what I mean.

Take Utah, a state I've fished plenty. Not long ago I was traveling east out of Salt Lake City. About two-hours' drive out, I noticed a river running alongside the road. It looked a little special to me, so I stopped at the next town, a little place called Duchesne.

I pulled up to the bank, cashed a check and asked to see the manager.

He was a pleasant man named Taylor and I introduced myself.

"I'm looking for some good fishing," I said. "How's that little river I passed coming up here?"

"That's the Duchesne River and it's marvelous," he said. "Plenty of rainbows and browns."

My eyes lit up.

"Actually we've got two good rivers in town—the Strawberry and the Duchesne," he explained. "Both have been a little sandy this week because of a little early-fall snowstorm we just had but they should clear up shortly. There's a stream a little out of town that's clear as a bell, though—Rock Creek. Would you be interested . . ."

I interrupted, "You're playing my song. Lead on."

Well, sir, that banker grabbed the telephone and called the game warden.

"He'll be happy to take you up there and show you around," Mr. Taylor said as he hung up.

And the game warden did. He spent most of the day with us, pointed out various mountains and gave us the names of streams and lakes that are seldom fished.

Rock Creek? Boy, it was wonderful—crystal clear and full of rainbow. I had myself some of the best fishing in months.

I thanked Mr. Taylor the next morning.

"Liked that, did you?" he said. "Well, the next time you're out in this country, give me a little notice. You can come out to my ranch and I guarantee you'll get your limit of nice browns in no time."

"Mister," I said, "it's a date."

I've already made plans to return there.

See what I'm getting at here? There's a surprise around every bend in this great country—state after state after state.

A man is never finished seeing it all—unless he kids himself into thinking he has and quits.

To my way of figuring, that's a sacrilege.

It's a great country out there chockfull of sights and experiences most men have never dreamed of. All a body has to do is get off his butt and look a bit.

And the more he sees, the more he realizes *he ain't seen nuthin' yet.*

54. If I Had One Week Left on Earth

A REPORTER ONCE ASKED: "GAD, IF THE ALMIGHTY SENT word that you had only one week left on earth, where would you go to fish for the last time?"

Well, sir, that's a good question—and a mighty tough question.

I've fished many, many wonderful spots in 63 years, more than any man deserves really. And I want to return to all of them.

Like:

Big Bird Island in Cape Cod's Buzzards Bay for those elusive schools of striped bass.

Flaming Gorge on the Green River in Utah for its game trout.

The Columbia River in Oregon for silver salmon that look like jewelry.

The Florida Keys for those rabbit-quick bone fish that spook so easily.

Among the Thousand Islands on the St. Lawrence River in northern New York and southern Ontario for bass and northern pike.

The Gulf of Mexico for Texas Kings and around the oil rigs for red snapper and lemon fish.

177

Around Hogg Island on Florida's St. John's River for bass.

Lake Atoka in Oklahoma for bass and catfish.

The Kennebec River in Maine for trout and bass—and on the Dead River, which flows into the Kennebec, for landlocked salmon, and squaretail, rainbow and brown trout.

Lakes Marion and Moultrie in South Carolina for stripers and bigmouth bass.

Off San Diego for albacore.

Glenwood Springs in Colorado, smack in the middle of trout country of the Colorado, Roaring Fork, Frying Pan, Crystal, Snow Mass and Eagle Rivers.

Black Lake region of Louisiana for bass.

Matane River in Quebec for Atlantic salmon.

Tennessee's Reelfoot and Kentucky Lakes and Greencove Reservoir for bass.

Lake Powell in Arizona for bass and trout.

Klamath River in California, near the Oregon border, for rainbows and browns.

Oswego River in New York for bass.

Grenada Lake in Mississippi for crappie and bass.

Jackson Hole in Wyoming for trout.

Deschutes River in Washington for rainbows and browns.

Mister, I could go on and on. That's just a slim fraction of the list. It'd be impossible to name them all. I haven't even included those dates I was telling you about on the west branch of the Salmon in Idaho and on the Duchesne in Utah.

And that's just it: I wouldn't even try to list them all because you can bet your boots I'd forget more than a couple.

Now let me get something crystal clear here. In no way am I suggesting that these are the best fishing spots in North America. That would be silly. As I've said, no man knows every stream and pond in this country, let alone this continent. I'm finding new ones every day. Besides, even if I could give a list of *my* favorites, who's to say it'd be best? After all, each man to his own taste.

All I'm saying is that these are a *few* of the places I hope to revisit some day.

If I could choose one—just one—for my last week on earth?

Well, sir, I guess it would be the Big Hole River up along Melrose, Montana, just south of Butte.

I'd pick the month of September and take along a horse to carry me to nice wadeable spots, a nice three-ounce 7' to 7'9" fly rod and a complete choice of dry flys.

Then I'd be in for the week of my life.

Why the Big Hole?

I can't answer that. I honestly can't. That big stream just fascinates me. I suppose it's the same as a man loving a good woman. He doesn't always know why and can't fully explain it. He just loves her and that's all there is to it. There's no one answer.

My love for Big Hole is something like that—a combination of a lot of reasons. Part of it is that it's a fabulous stream—fast, mirror-clear and brimming with fat, sassy browns and rainbows. Another reason is that going for trout —particularly with a dry fly—is my favorite kind of fishing.

But my attraction for the Big Hole has to be more than those two reasons because, as good as it is, there are other trout streams just as good.

I guess what clinches it for me is the Big Hole's atmosphere. It sits in gorgeous country—smack in the middle of the Rockies.

That's important to me. It goes along with my view on what fishing really is—the whole picture. It's more than catching a few fish. It's soaking up nature and all its marvelous wonders too. A man waits on a fish and has a chance to see all the world going on around him: the trees, the wind, the birds, the rushing stream—even the insects. It's all alive and he's part of it.

179

So that's the Big Hole—all of these things rolled into one. Yes, sir, that's how I'd spend my last week on earth if I could choose it.

Now I can't guarantee I'll ever get to heaven. But give me that one solid week, brother, and I'd be halfway there.

55. *I've Been a Lucky Cuss*

A YEAR OR SO AGO, WE WERE FILMING A SHOW OUT OF Hurricane Dock on Tennessee's Greencove Reservoir.

I had a wonderful teen-ager named Billy handling my boat. He was a tall and courteous lad—and an inquisitive one. That boy must have asked me a hundred and one questions during the four or five days we were on location. They weren't obnoxious questions—just the natural and innocent ones of a curious youngster who had never been out of the hill country.

After wrapping up the filming, Bob Kimball and I began driving to the Cooksville airport. All of a sudden that cameraman began chuckling.

"What's tickling you, Bob?" I asked.

"That Billy," he said, shaking his head.

"What do you mean?" I asked.

"As you were packing up this morning, he was raving about you—marveling at all the things you know and have done," Bob explained. "Then he stopped, thought a second, and blurted out: 'You know, that Gad must be a hundred and fifty years old!'"

Well, sir, I thought that was priceless.

A hundred and fifty, huh? I don't feel a day over thirty-five!

There's a lot of truth in that old saw about a man being as old as he feels. And I feel I have a lot of living ahead of me.

In a way, I didn't want to write this book. When a man tells about his life, he's dealing in the past. And what's happened in the past doesn't interest me. Only the future does.

I always look ahead, not behind.

What happened last week doesn't mean a darn. What's going to happen next week—that's what I am interested in.

I'm always looking for new experiences. And the more challenging the better. Like last year when I went out and began taking organ lessons. A lot of people thought that was downright funny.

"A little late to be starting, isn't it, Gad?" They laughed.

No, sir, it isn't. It's never too late.

I had been booting my backside about ever since I quit taking piano lessons as a kid. As I got older I developed a love for piano and organ music and realized what I had passed up. So I finally did something about it.

If there's anything in this world I want to do, I do it. I hate the word "can't." I really do. It rubs against my grain. A man can do just about anything he wants if he sets his mind to it. That's always been my motto and I'm not going to stop living by it now just because I'm seventy.

Age has very little to do with it.

Sure I've been lucky. I've always enjoyed excellent health and have had very few sick days in my life. So I've been ahead of the game physically.

But age is as much mental as it is physical.

I hope I never get like some of my friends who are living in the past. They think they're all through, just because they've passed age sixty-five. Don't try to sell me that. A man is done only when he feels he's done.

"Gad, remember the time you and I . . ." they start to say.

"Never mind what we *did!*" I interrupt. "Let's concentrate on what we're *going* to do!"

I like to remember and think about past experiences up to a point, but I've got plans mapped for years to come.

Whether or not I'll get to them is something only the good Lord knows. It's all in His hands. I realize nothing and nobody lasts forever in this world, and that I could be gone tomorrow.

That doesn't disturb me. I've had a full and fascinating life. There's nothing I'd rather have been, and I don't think I've missed much. It's been a happy life, full of the two joys that please me most: rambling and fishing.

Yes, sir, I'm an extremely fortunate man.

I'm not talking about my television success. Sure it's nice to have a national show, to get 13,000 letters in a week; to have people recognize that Borsalino sitting on my head as I walk down a street and to have the honor of endorsing tackle. Everyone likes to be liked.

But I'm talking about the important things in life—the *really* important things. I've never felt better. Dad passed away in 1934 and mom in 1946, but I've been blessed that the Lord has kept the rest of the gang in tip-top health too.

They're all in the pink: wife Ruby; brother Ray in Denver; and all my sisters—Mrs. Lillian Hesler in Greenup, Illinois; Mrs. Irene Sacco in Decatur, Illinois; and Mrs. Dorothy Jacoway in Denver. The same goes for a small army of nieces and nephews and grandnieces and grandnephews.

Yes, sir, I've been a lucky cuss—extremely lucky.

When the good Lord does call me, I'll have no complaints —only appreciation for how well He's done by me all these years.

In the meantime, though, I'm not going to sit around and wait. Time is wasting. There're miles to travel, places to see and fish to catch.

A hundred and fifty years old, eh, Billy? Okay, boy, you look me up around year 2046.

I just might be still gaddin' about.